A Bible Study for Church Repentance

SACKCLOTH AND ASHES OF THE HEART

SHERI CARUSO

First Printed in the United States of America, 2019.

Second Edition, Capture Books

©2021 (revised)

Capture Books, Imprint Sheri Caruso

All Rights Reserved

5856 S. Lowell Blvd. Ste 32–202

Littleton, Colorado 80123

720–210–7107

ISBN 13: 978-1-951084-42-4 paperback

ISBN 13: 978-1-951084-45-5 ePub-Kindle

ENDORSEMENTS

Reviews:

"Great study! Powerful, at times gut-wrenching, always thought provoking. Prompted me to truly examine my walk with God. Revealed to me where I had allowed complacency and compromise to creep in and obscure my relationship with God. Inspired me to draw closer to God daily. My prayer life changed and my Christian walk became stronger. I am no longer inclined to compromise on what I believe and value."

— Stephanie W.

Capture Books

In loving memory of my Dad,
Rev. Joseph L Comer Sr.
You taught your children the ways of God; His love,
grace and mercy. The seeds you planted have grown into
ripened fruit and will multiply beyond comprehension.
I wish you were here to see the fruits of your labor.
You are loved and truly missed.

Preface

My husband's words, "You have nothing good to say. . ." resonated in my mind as I began to write this study. Who am I to write a Bible study as crucial as this? Who am I to speak to others? Who am I that the Lord has entrusted?

Before we go any further and before you begin to judge my husband's words, I must tell you the rest of his comment, "but God does."

My husband uttered these wise words after I'd confided in him right before a speaking engagement. I was nervous, worried and wondered if my words would have any meaning to the ears that were to hear. This wasn't my first speaking engagement, nor will it be my last. Why this one brought on such insecurities was beyond my understanding, but God knew.

God knew he was going to use my husband to speak words of wisdom and comfort. God knew those words would resonate in my mind every time He placed a call on my heart.

But God does...

This is not the first Bible study I've written, nor will it be my last. I've learned a very important lesson as a Woman's Ministry Leader throughout the years - when God says...YOU do!

When God gives me direction for our team, I lead. When God places a burden on my heart, I pray. When God gives me discernment, I acknowledge. When God places a Bible study on my heart, I write.

I felt this study was beyond my scope, beyond my understanding, beyond me and to be honest, it is, but not for God.

I prayed and studied and fretted but as soon as my fingers touched the keyboard, the words just came.

We must look past our abilities, place all our trust in the Lord, pray for His will to be done and then ACT. *God* does act, then!

My heart is burdened, deeply burdened for the state of the 'Church'; I mean the global Church of Christ. Worldly views, desires and needs have seeped into the cracks of our pulpits and congregations. They have begun to reshape the hearts and actions of believers.

But that 'new' shape doesn't resemble Christ.

When asking the Lord what direction I should lead the women, I could not shake the feeling that repentance is a topic that is vital to our relationship with the Lord. Not just "Lord I'm sorry, forgive me" repentance, but deep-down sorrow that would be life-changing; we needed a study on spiritual renewal where we learned what was wrong, what could be, and then a time to do personal business with the Lord.

The women embraced this study, and I began to see changes in their walk with Christ. Just as the gentiles are to provoke jealousy amongst the Jews, the men within our church wanted what the women received so they began the study as well.

Since that time, I've noticed a renewed spirit within our local church, a spirit of restoration and a spirit of rejuvenation.

That is the purpose behind offering this study to the broader Church; to restore the Church of Christ by reviving our hearts with a supernatural love, giving us strength in a world full of evil, realigning our doctrine back to truth, exposing evil within our congregation, keeping us connected to God's headship, teaching us to be faithful followers regardless of our situation and instill God's character in every aspect of our lives.

In this 8–week study we will look at the seven churches in Revelation. We will reveal who Jesus is, explore His commendations, correlate the charges Jesus had against the 7 churches to the churches of today, heed his warnings and the action we must take so we can stay the course and receive the rewards Jesus has for all those who overcome.

There are daily prayers of repentance throughout this study. After all, the focus of this study is – to reveal, repent and restore.

Are you ready? Are you truly ready for Jesus' return? Take this journey of repentance with us and be restored!

Acknowledgements

I would be amiss to not first and foremost acknowledge the Lord Jesus Christ through His Holy Spirit for making this Bible study possible. It's only by divine will that I was granted the ability, wisdom and means to accomplish such a task. I relied faithfully on the Lord and bathed each word in prayer while writing this study. I am truly humbled and honored that the Lord entrusted me with a project of this magnitude, I have gained so much personal insight during the process.

Many thanks belong to the ladies in our Solid Rock Christian Fellowship's Women Bible study (Stephanie, Paula, Nancy, Heather, Jennifer, Dee, Nan, and Donna (who is now with the Lord)) for your encouragement and willingness to be the first group to experience the benefits of this repentance study.

To my pastor Rev. Bill Woods for your advice, tutelage, and support – I truly value your leadership as well as your friendship. Pastor Bill Woods, you have been a huge support and I thank you for advocating this study to all your acquaintances and colleagues in Christ.

A special thank you to my brother Rev. Joe Comer Jr. for reviewing this study to ensure its credibility with the word of God as well as the hours you spent editing. Although your schedule is full you still took the time to assist your little sister with this project.

Tonya Blessings, thank you for identifying the need for this study throughout the body of Christ and introducing me to Capture Books. It was the Lord's plan for you to pick up this book and get the process started so many others can reap the benefits of this study.

Thank you, Laura Bartnick, for your willingness to publish this book and for your guidance during the process. Thank you for your creative vision and talent. Also thank you to the many talented Capture Books editors for your expertise in editing this book, you have done an exceptional job.

I also want to thank my husband Joe Caruso for his support, patience and understanding during those endless hours of studying and writing; especially the numerous 2 am inspirational writing sessions.

To my Mom, Jennifer Comer, your assistance in design and structure as well as your support was hugely beneficial. Thank you for always believing in me and encouraging me to continue working for the Lord.

Finally, I want to thank YOU, the reader. I want to thank you for understanding the need for repentance, and for having a desire to make a change within the body of Christ, as well as your nation. I commend you for your dedication and encourage you to continue running the race for Christ.

Chapter One

Preservation

**"Restore us, O God; Cause your face to shine,
and we shall be saved!"**
Psalms 80:3 NKJV

Fashion is such a peculiar social statement.

Many fashion idiosyncrasies have been ushered into society throughout history. Some fashion ideas were outright ridiculous, yet there were fashion designs that became innovative and trendy.

Fashions such as tennis shoes and blue jeans escaped cultural trends and became stylish staples. Other creative inventions, like zippers and buttons, changed the fashion industry forever.

Though the majority of clothing; styles, name brands, and accessories, has evolved and improved life as we know it, we can't forget about the barbaric and deadly fashion trends from the past.

Some examples are feet binding, corsets, stiff collars, mad hatters and lead paint. Yes, we've learned from the past. Fashion is trendy not deadly. Or, is it?

There's a difference between fashion trends and fashion statements. Trends are seasonal styles that shape our wardrobe whereas fashion statements declare a belief, emotion, or mindset. Fashion statements aren't necessarily negative, but they are influential. It's safe to say that most people will base an opinion of someone by the way they are dressed.

For instance, if you see someone dressed in all black with dark makeup and greasy hair, you would think they are depressed or distraught.

Let's say you saw someone in a cowboy hat and boots; you'd possibly think they're from the country. How about dirty clothes, messy hair and holes in their shoes? Would homeless cross your mind?

What if you saw someone walking around barefoot, dressed in sackcloth, and smeared in ashes from head to toe? Would you think they're a little bizarre, unconventional or idiosyncratic? Maybe "off their rocker" comes to mind?

This may be true in society today, but in Biblical times, dressing in sackcloth was a common way to reveal a heart condition. Not a medical heart condition, but as a religious declaration proclaiming an emotional state of the heart such as grief, anger, shock, lament, or shame.

Throughout the Old Testament we find countless examples of people tearing their clothes and/or putting on sackcloth and ashes.

- Job put on sackcloth and ashes (dust) (Job 16:15) to mourn, while wrestling with his Maker and his friends about God's justice in whether Job deserved his suffering.
- David mourned the death of Abner, the commander of Saul's army (2 Samuel 3:31).
- Jacob tore his clothes and put on sackcloth as he mourned for his son Joseph (Genesis 37:34).
- Mordecai tore his clothes, put on sackcloth and ashes and walked around the city "wailing loudly and bitterly" when he saw the plans to kill the Jews (Esther 4:1).

A few others mentioned in the Bible are:

- Daniel (Daniel 9:3)
- Eliakim (2 Kings 19:2)
- King Ahab (1 Kings 21:27)
- King Hezekiah (Isaiah 37:1)
- The elders of Jerusalem (Lamentations 2:10)

What does this fashion statement mean? Why were people tearing their clothes, putting on scratchy garments and dirtying themselves with dust and ashes? To understand why, let's look at the symbolism for each action, starting with the tearing of clothes.

TEARING CLOTHES

In biblical times, it was customary for people to rip their clothing to express strong emotions due to tragic events or situations. This act was not only a public display of grief, shame, or anger — it was sacrificial. Clothing was expensive back then. Factories weren't around for mass production; instead, each garment was laboriously manufactured by hand and produced according to the need.

We can therefore assume the average person didn't own a large wardrobe like we do today; they most likely owned only a few outfits. When a person tore their clothes, it demonstrated how distraught or grieved they were. Destroying an expensive necessity in those days would most likely be equivalent to us destroying one of our "comfort" household items (TV's, couches, beds, dishwasher, washing machine etc.) to display our grief.

SACKCLOTH

Sackcloth was an uncomfortable and scratchy material most commonly made from black goat's hair. It's believed to be woven from a combination of other fibers such as camel hair, hemp and cotton. Sackcloth was meant to be abrasive and unattractive, a constant reminder of why a person would don such a garment.

It was an outward sign of mourning, humility, sincere repentance, simplicity and being spiritually poor.

ASHES/DUST

Ashes or dust was an outward sign of mourning, humility, and repentance.

Ashes are still used today in some religions. They're a reminder that we were made from dust and we shall return to dust. It can also be an outward sign that we need to turn away from our sinful nature and be faithful to the Gospel. Some religious traditions use Ash Wednesday to signify this idea.

Combined, tearing one's clothes and putting on sackcloth & ashes, was an outward sign of a person's heart. Those who adorned sackcloth and ashes also had another fundamental element, an inward sign of repentance. Prayer and fasting are important aspects in manifesting our true heart and intentions. They are an inward display of humility, mourning and repentance.

The entire city of Nineveh was spared because the people recognized their sin and showed true repentance. Everyone from the king down to the common person put on sackcloth, fasted and prayed. Even the animals, herds and flock, fasted and wore sackcloth. (Jonah 3:6–9)

Nineveh was not a small country town; it was an influential metropolis with an estimated population of 120,000 people. It took three days to walk around the entire city of Nineveh. (Jonah 3:3)

With its size and influence in mind, we need to understand and recognize that EVERYONE in Nineveh repented of their sins. With a city that size, there is bound to be division and evil dominion.

Nineveh was an important religious center for worshipping Ishtar, the goddess associated with love, beauty, sex, desire, fertility, war, justice, and political power. Nineveh was the capital of Assyria.

The Assyrians were cruel people who showed no mercy and were a constant thorn to Israel. Nineveh rejected God, worshipped idols and committed many horrible sins — yet God spared them from destruction because of their sincere repentance. God paid attention and knew the true condition of their heart; He extended grace and mercy towards them.

Can you imagine the impact if our cities, states and countries as a whole would sincerely repent of their sins, ask for forgiveness and depart from their evil ways?

The world today is evil, most likely just as evil if not more than Nineveh or Sodom & Gomorrah. We've not only allowed and accepted this evilness into our society but it has begun to penetrate our churches as well. John Wesley was once asked if he feared the Methodist church in America would cease to exist.

"Never!" he replied. *"But,"* he added, *"I am fearful that it will cease to exist as a movement with power and godliness and become only a church with a form of godliness, denying the power thereof."*

Well folks, John Wesley's fears were justified but not just for the Methodist church. ALL Christian denominations are afflicted with this lack of power and godliness. They portray themselves to be righteous but deny God's power and truth. Yes, the Christian Church is knee-deep in idolatry, adultery, sexual sin, complacency, unforgiving hearts, thievery, lies and even the omission of God, heaven, hell, Jesus, and the work on the cross.

Church, the hour of Jesus' return is drawing near and it's time we become distraught over our condition. It's time we become uncomfortable sitting in our padded pews and prostrate ourselves before the Lord. Do we want to see change? Change in our lives, change in our congregation, change in our cities and nations? It's time to tear apart what we hold more valuable than God. It's time we mourn and humble ourselves before the Lord. It's time we repent and have a sincere heart before God.

Does this mean we should walk around with our heads hung low as we wail in the streets? Does it mean we put on old, uncomfortable scratchy clothes while we pour buckets of ashes on our heads? It might do us well to go back to the Old Testament practice of sackcloth and ashes, but this is more about changing our heart condition and not pharisaical displays.

Our intent is not to be trendy in the Christian community, nor is it to draw attention to ourselves.

Our intent is to draw God's attention to our broken hearts.

Symbolically putting on sackcloth and ashes within our heart means we adorn humility. We inwardly and sincerely mourn for our sins. We come to the understanding that we are mere dust and acknowledge how mighty our God is. We spend time in the Lord's presence as we spend time on our knees. We praise and thank God for He has granted us grace and mercy.

This study will take us through the revelations, praises, accusations, requirements, warnings, and encouragement Jesus gave to the seven churches in Revelation. The churches and their controversies are just as real today as they were back then. We will begin to recognize where we, the individual Christian, and the church as a whole, are guilty of the same pronouncements Jesus gave the seven churches in Revelation.

This study will walk us through steps of true repentance, to overcome a sinful nature and create a more dynamic relationship with the Lord. In each chapter we will look at a different church. We will identify the revelation of Jesus, the accusation Jesus had against the church, the action He requires of us and encouragement for the overcomer. At the end of each chapter there are specific prayer focuses, one for each day of the week. Remember, this is a study of repentance.

This study is for groups or individuals. You can focus on each church weekly and follow the prayer focus daily. There is also an option to follow one prayer focus for an entire week. However you or your group decides to follow this study, do it consistently so as not to fall away from the essence of repentance.

Through this study you are encouraged to do some type of fasting. Since this is a minimal 8–week study, it isn't encouraged or recommended to completely fast every meal until you finish the study. Instead, you could fast one meal a day — such as lunch or fast a nonfood item like social media or television. Those with medical conditions are encouraged to do a non-nutrition fast.

WARNING

You will most likely experience spiritual warfare during this time. Stay alert and don't lose heart, God will surely take notice.

This first chapter will prepare you for the study to come. Take time to truly pray from the heart with daily diligence.

"And shall God not avenge His own elect who cry out day and night to Him, though He bears long with them? I tell you that He will avenge them speedily. Nevertheless, when the Son of Man comes, will He really find faith on the earth?" Luke 18:7–8 NKJV

DAY ONE - PRAYER FOCUS

Pray for protection! Protection from enemy attacks and anything that will distract, disengage, or discourage you from this study.

Scripture References:
2 Thessalonians 3:3
Psalm 59:1
Psalm 140:4

DAY TWO - PRAYER FOCUS

Pray that the lies of the enemy will be revealed whether those lies have placed a veil over your eyes or the eyes of others. Pray against those lies and ask for the willingness to accept the truth despite the lies that have veiled your own eyes.

Scripture References:
Jeremiah 9:5–6
Ephesians 6:12
Ephesians 5:13

DAY THREE - PRAYER FOCUS

Pray that God will reveal your heart during this study. Let all that is hidden come to light.

Scripture References:
Psalms 139:23–24
Luke 12:2
Jeremiah 17:10

DAY FOUR - PRAYER FOCUS

Pray for wisdom and understanding. Pray that God reveals His desire and will to you.

Scripture References:
James 1:5
Proverbs 4:6–7
Proverbs 19:20

DAY FIVE - PRAYER FOCUS

Pray for discernment. Pray to hear the Lord's voice and to recognize when the enemy is attempting to infiltrate your heart, mind or actions.

Scripture References:
Leviticus 10:10
Psalms 119:66
Psalms 92:11

DAY SIX - PRAYER FOCUS

Pray for change and revival. Pray for consistent change, that you will never be complacent or satisfied with the ordinary.

Scripture References:
Isaiah 43:19
Psalms 85:6
Psalms 80:19

DAY SEVEN - PRAYER FOCUS

Pray for more presence and power from the Holy Spirit.

Scripture References:
1 Chronicles 16:11
Galatians 5:25
Psalms 143:6

Chapter Two

Revive our Hearts

"My soul clings to the dust;
Revive me according to Your word."
Psalms 119:25 NJKV

God, the creator of all things, the maker of the heavens and earth, formed man and personally breathed life into him.

God, the creator of all things, the maker of the heavens and earth, had compassion on man and made him a mate; together man and woman are mankind.

God, the creator of all things, the maker of the heavens and earth, gave mankind food to eat and a beautiful garden to live in.

God, the creator of all things, the maker of the heavens and earth, walked in the garden to fellowship with mankind.

God thought of us, each and every one of us, throughout existence. God's thoughts dwell on us. God's plans for us were laid out before the foundations of the earth. God desires good things for us. God gave his son for us.

You may not feel loved. You may be dealing with disappointment, pain, loss or hardships. You may feel like an outsider, unwanted or unworthy. You may be angry or depressed. Your past may have been turmoil and you feel your future is uncertain. Regardless of how you feel or what you think, know this:

You were created out of love.
You are designed to love.
You're loved.

Genesis tells us that God created us in His image. 1 John 4:7–11 tells us that God IS love. Since we're created in His image, we are designed to love. With that said, let's look at the church of Ephesus - the church that forsook its first love.

REVELATION OF JESUS

"To the angel of the church of Ephesus write, 'These things says He who holds the seven stars in His right hand, who walks in the midst of the seven golden lampstands:" Revelation 2:1 NKJV

Jesus is the one who walks in the midst of the churches. He knows our success, failures, problems, needs, deeds and victories. He is the watchman and will judge the actions of the church. He is the commander for the Angels of the church. Jesus is also the encourager and the One Who lifts our heads.

COMMENDATION

"I know your works, your labor, your patience, and that you cannot bear those who are evil. And you have tested those who say they are apostles and are not, and have found them liars; and you have persevered and have patience, and have labored for My name's sake and have not become weary." Revelation 2:2–3 NKJV

Jesus says well done for all your hard work for His name's sake. You haven't complained or grown tired of ministry work. You've reached out and done many good works for the Lord.

You've become Bereans of God's word and are able to discern the truth and call out false teachings/teachers. You know the difference between good and evil. You do not condone evil nor do you compromise God's standards and allow evil to seep into the congregation.

"But this you have, that you hate the deeds of the Nicolaitans, which I also hate." Revelation 2:6 NKJV

You recognize and hate corrupt and abominable practices. You do not allow those practices to infiltrate the congregation or your heart.

THE CHARGE

"Nevertheless I have this against you, that you have left your first love." Revelation 2:4 NKJV

You've lost your zeal for God. The tenderness of God's grace and mercy has grown cold in your heart. The seriousness of your relationship with God has become stale. Instead of doing work in love and compassion, you do them out of obligation.

No longer do you praise and worship God daily and seek His face.

Your consistent love has become:

1. Occasional Love – Only when you can remember to love or when something good happens.

2. Circumstantial Love – Only when you really need God to move or respond to a situation.

3. Guarded Love – You've set limits on how much you can love God and how much you allow God to love you.

4. <u>Superficial Love</u> – You speak it with your mouth and actions but there's a disconnection between your mouth, hands and heart.

5. <u>Complacent love</u> – The love you claim to have for God has become self-gratifying. You've become conceited, self-righteous and self-satisfied.

ACTION NEEDED

"Remember therefore from where you have fallen; repent and do the first works," Revelation 2:5a NKJV

Remember the depths of your sin. Never forget the price paid for your salvation. Humble yourself before the Lord and ask for forgiveness. Show proof of your commitment to Christ. Make a change so that your deeds produce righteous results.

Concentrate on the Lord's will and perform excellence in His power. Do not distract yourself with the world. Set yourself apart. Focus on the Lord's purpose with prayer and perseverance.

WARNING

"or else I will come to you quickly and remove your lampstand from its place-unless you repent." Revelation 2:5b NKJV

If you do not earnestly repent and change, the light of Christ in your life will quickly be extinguished.

ENCOURAGEMENT FOR THE OVERCOMER

"He who has an ear, let him hear what the Spirit says to the churches. To him who overcomes I will give to eat from the

tree of life, which is in the midst of the Paradise of God." Revelation 2:7 NKJV

Those that recognize the error of their ways, humble themselves, repent and do what the Lord requires of them, will be able to commune with God. They will be given the gift of eternal life. They will not be separated from God but given all that is promised in Heaven.

Reviving our hearts may seem easy for some while others may not know where to begin. Although it's in God's nature to always love, regardless of our actions, mankind is fickle, easily distracted, discouraged and stubborn.

As humans we need to understand "why" we fall out of love in order to revive the love we've seemingly misplaced.

HAVE TO'S – WANT TO'S

Our "want-to's" feel like our "have-to's", don't they?

- You used to "want-to" talk about Jesus. Maybe you've had some disappointments and now, you feel like you "have-to" love God and put mentions in about Him in conversations since that's what the Bible says. You've allowed your "want-to" to change because of worldly circumstances.

- You use to "want-to" praise and worship the Lord but after a while the songs of praise have lost their meaning. Your "want-to" has turned into a monotonous "have-to".

- You used to "want-to" pray and just talk with God. You were so excited when God moved mountains and thrilled to just speak with God. Lately you have been wallowing in the desert. You've lost heart but you know you still "have-to" pray. Making room for prayer in your schedule, hanging out with God, talking all night with Abba Father and pleasing the Lord, now feels like a requirement instead of a desire.

SETTLING SEDIMENT

Sometimes we tend to settle into the habitual act of love without realizing we fell out of love in the first place. It's become a way of life instead a way TO life. You're habitual and obligatory Christian lifestyle has settled at the bottom of the well and hardened; it's unmovable.

You're not being lifted up in the bucket of life-giving water used to revive the soul. Instead, your heart is being eroded away by the obligatory lifestyle. If not revived, the sediment will eventually accumulate, creating layers of unusable debris.

POLITICAL POINTERS

You begin to find fault in God when God doesn't move the way you want him to or when God doesn't provide what you feel you need.

This is when you begin to point your finger at God and say, "It's all your fault". When you see others hurt and suffering, you wonder where God is. You don't consult the Lord, nor do you search His word for answers. You give up. You may not vocalize it, but God knows what you internalize in your heart.

We fail to realize that God works in mysterious ways; we are to place our faith and trust in Him. We also fail to recognize that we are in charge of our own decisions and choices. When we're not walking in step with Christ, we lose our way. Have we unforgiving hearts for the very one <u>Who</u> freely forgives us... and often?

ORDINARY ORTHODOX

Ordinary Christian life settles in and you've lost excitement in the relationship. You've told yourself; I'm a Christian and that's it. There are no new revelations and no adoring thoughts about Jesus.

You've become complacent. You're comfortable. You're stale. Your efforts are lackadaisical. You don't put much thought into who God is, what he's done or where you are in the scheme of things.

Where is your heart attitude taking you?

You asked for forgiveness, you go to church, you're faithful with tithes, you read the Bible, you do good things and you're nice to others.

You're an all-around 'good person' superstar. "What else is there?" you wonder.

What else isn't there? God has so much to offer, we just have to open our eyes, hearts and minds to all that he has planned for us.

GUILTY GLUTTON

What you once craved in your relationship with God has turned into stale bread. Instead of being fed, you settle for spoiled milk. You left God out too long and now the relationship has spoiled. You're empty and then guilt begins to fill you. The more you eat the guilt, the fatter you become. The fatter you become, the less you move. The less you move, the greater the likelihood you will die.

You know you shouldn't feel this way, but you do. Doubt creeps in. Did you even mean it when you asked Jesus into your life? Were you lying to God? To yourself? Were you pretending all along? Were you ever saved? Did God even care? Does God know?

You doubt yourself and then you begin to doubt God. You doubt your position, your ability, your effectiveness, your testimony or your salvation.

Love isn't something you do out of obligation. Love isn't condemnation.

We love simply because he loved us first. 1 John 4:19

God, the creator of all things, the maker of the heavens and earth, created us….to LOVE.

"Though I speak with the tongues of men and of angels, but have not love, I have become a sounding brass or a clanging cymbal. And though I have the gift of prophecy, and understand all mysteries and all knowledge, and though I have all faith, so that I could remove mountains, but have not love, I am nothing. And though I bestow all my goods to feed the poor, and though I give my body to be burned, but have not love, it profits me nothing." 1 Corinthians 13:1–3 NKJV

DAY ONE - PRAYER FOCUS

Repent for not following the most important commandment of all – to love the Lord your God with all your heart, soul and mind.

Ask the Lord to show you how to love. Thank the Lord for looking beyond your faults and loving you unconditionally. Ask the Lord to revive your heart with a supernatural love that only comes from Him. Ask for eyes to see and a heart to love as Jesus loves.

Scripture References:
1 John 3:1–2
1 John 4:16
Colossians 3:14

DAY TWO - PRAYER FOCUS

Repent for not loving others as Christ has loved us. Repent for your unforgiving heart to those who have wronged you.

Ask the Lord to help you see what real love is, for your neighbor and the stranger on the street. Ask God to give you the same compassion that He has for people. Ask for a heart to love those who are difficult to love.

Scripture References:
2 Timothy 2:23–26
Romans 12:10
John 15:12

DAY THREE - PRAYER FOCUS

Repent for not loving yourself. Repent for the negative and harmful words you have said about yourself and to yourself.

Ask the Lord to transform your heart and to reveal how much he loves you. Ask for understanding on how marvelous you are. Ask the Lord to curb your tongue and speak life into yourself and those around you.

Scripture References:
Ephesians 5:29
Jeremiah 29:11
Romans 5:8

DAY FOUR - PRAYER FOCUS

Repent for not hearing the cries of the brokenhearted and for not loving them as Jesus has called us to do.

Ask the Lord to show you how to have compassion on those whose spirits are crushed. Ask for a heart to love those that the world has forsaken because Jesus died for them as well.

Scripture References:
1 Samuel 16:7
Psalms 34:18
Psalms 147:3

DAY FIVE- PRAYER FOCUS

Repent for complaining about circumstances and having a bad attitude. Ask the Lord to fill your heart and mouth with positivity.

Ask him to change your heart when you have a bad attitude and close your mouth before you spew negative comments. Ask for your heart to be revived with love no matter the circumstance.

Scripture References:
1 Thessalonians 5:16–18
Colossians 4:6
Proverbs 15:4

DAY SIX- PRAYER FOCUS

Repent for becoming stagnant. Repent for not allowing the spirit of God to penetrate your life.

Ask the Holy Spirit to fill your heart with love and joy unspeakable. Have the Lord be the lifter of your head and reveal himself to you.

Scripture References:
John 15:4
Psalms 3:3
Psalms 16:11

DAY SEVEN - PRAYER FOCUS

Repent for allowing obligation to be your heart instead of love.

Ask God to be the center of everything you do. God is love therefore you will operate in love. Let the Lord know how much you love Him and ask Him to help you to love Him more every day. Ask for a desire to never be full and to always want more love in your heart, love for God, love for yourself and love for others.

Scripture References:
1 John 3:18
Matthew 6:21
Psalms 40:8

Chapter Three

Give us Strength

**"Yes, and all who desire to live a godly life
in Christ Jesus will suffer persecution."**
2 Timothy 3:12 MEV

Imagine this:

A mother and father are reading the Bible to their children and teaching them the truth about Jesus Christ and his promises. Seems comforting and sounds encouraging, doesn't it?

You can probably picture it in your mind:

A family of four just finished a delicious and satisfying meal. Afterwards, they clean up together and retire to the living room. Mom and Dad sit on the couch while their son and daughter sit on the floor in front of them, eagerly awaiting tonight's discussion about Jesus. Dad flips through the Bible on the coffee table as he reads the devotion. The discussion is joyful and encouraging. Everyone smiles as the children give their Mom and Dad a huge hug before heading upstairs to bed. Sounds a little 'Leave it to Beaverish', doesn't it?

Before we continue, let's look at the rest of the story and no, it isn't about the average American Christian family. This story is about the reality of a family in an impoverished country, a country that has outlawed Christianity. It's a country riddled with terrorists looking for a reason to kill and destroy. It's Satan's domain.

So imagine this:

A mother and father are reading the Bible to their children and teaching them the truth about Jesus Christ and His promises behind locked doors. They are fearful of others knowing they're Christians. The parents also know they are running out of time to teach their children the truth since terrorist activity is increasing at an alarming rate. The children are taught about Christ's love for all mankind and about his grace and mercy. They learn how important salvation is and to be obedient to Christ regardless of intimidation from terrorist groups.

They are also taught about forgiveness — how important it is for their children to forgive others regardless of how terrible a person may be. It's time. The parents need to prepare their children for the reality soon to come.

One day the parents sat their children down and told them about the possibility of a terrorist breaking down the door, intending to cause harm. They instruct their children that no matter what the terrorist did, the children were to tell the terrorist that they forgive them. The parents told the children that under NO circumstance were they to denounce Jesus as their Lord and Savior. Several days later, as the family sat peacefully inside their home, there was a loud boom at the front door. The next thing they knew, the room was filled with people dressed in black with their faces covered. All they could see was the sinister look in the stranger's eyes as they waved rifles in the air.

There was a lot of yelling going on as the strangers tied the family up. They placed the children in front of their parents to scare and intimidate them. The children were forced to watch these strangers beat their parents for no apparent reason. The strangers then went to the children and began to ask them questions about their allegiance. Would they denounce Christ and follow them? They yelled and screamed, but the children didn't waiver.

Then, the strangers threatened the children; if they didn't denounce Christ and pledge their allegiance to them, they would kill their parents. The children still didn't waiver. The strangers proceeded to behead their parents right in front of them.

As the children cried, the strangers asked them again "Will you pledge your allegiance to us?" The children dried their tears and looked into those sinister eyes. With sincerity and confidence, they said "I forgive you and Jesus loves you." Sadly, the entire family is slaughtered.

"If the world hates you, you know that it hated Me before it hated you." John 15:18 MEV

How would you fare as the parent in this situation? How would you fare as the child? Would you have the strength to love these people and exclaim Jesus' love for them? Would you be able to hold on to the truth without wavering? What is truth, anyways?

"And we know that the Son of God has come and has given us understanding, so that we may know Him who is true, and we are in Him who is true — His Son Jesus Christ. He is the true God and eternal life." 1 John 5:20 MEV

Jesus is truth. Jesus is the Son of God. Jesus is the true God. Jesus is eternal life – no one can have eternal life without Jesus.

The world will always fight against truth. Truth is light. Light expels that which is wrong. This is a fallen world whose ruler is the prince of darkness and master of deception. The world as a whole denies the fact that there is an absolute truth. Why?

1. We've idolized humanity, deeming ourselves all-knowing instead of God.

2. We don't feel truth blends well with what we desire.

3. Everyone has their own idea of truth, most of which is through popular opinion.

4. If there's no scientific reasoning, then truth is not possible. There is a cause and effect for everything in science, which eliminates the possibility of a greater being such as God, who can do the impossible.

5. Truth does not fall into our agenda.

6. Satan has come to steal and destroy all that God has created and loved.

The world has begun to apologize for truth, to bend the truth, to deny truth, to redefine truth, to offend the truth. Truth is truth.

Truth doesn't require a defense, it requires exclamation!

The world will continue to persecute those who believe and live in truth –they can't handle the truth. Granted, the majority of the world doesn't currently experience the reality of persecution such as the story in the beginning of this lesson. Certain countries like America have been noted as experiencing "polite persecution," which some feel is not worthy of being called persecution at all.

Persecution is generally and simply defined as: Hostility and ill-treatment, especially because of race or political or religious beliefs. Persistent annoyance or harassment.

Persecution is not defined as torturing and murdering those who hold a belief differing from yours. Is it still persecution? Absolutely, but it isn't the only means of persecution. Christians around the world are continuously treated in an ill manner. There's an obvious hostility towards the church and they are persistently harassed. The world is annoyed with Christianity.

Jesus told us this would be the case, but it isn't our job to make nicey-nice and not offend.

Jesus even said he didn't come into this world to make friends but to divide the believers from the enemies, truth from deception. (Matthew 10:34–39). The war on Christianity (polite persecution) has greatly changed the landscape of righteousness and the message throughout our society and in our churches.

- Prayer and even the mention of God have been eradicated from our schools, yet they're willing to teach about other religions that defy Christ.
- Confusion about our sexual identity is an agenda designed to devalue God's creation of man and woman. It's been pushed into our society and in our schools. People no longer know whether to call themselves a male or a female.
- Restrooms are becoming non-gender and to fight against this agenda is considered discrimination and a crime in some areas.
- Same-sex relationship is another agenda designed to destroy the sanctity of marriage as designed by God.
- Abortion has become a political format and its agenda gives women a false sense of superiority. Women now believe they have the right to determine if a human being lives or dies. God is the only one with the authority for life and death. (1 Samuel 2:6)
- People want to destroy evidence of Godly morals by tearing down displays of the Ten Commandments, taking God out of constitutions and discrediting Christian organizations yet they are allowing statues of Satan to stand tall.
- Hyper-grace has infiltrated our pulpits and congregations. This unbiblical theory lets people live like the world and yet consider themselves part of the Kingdom of God. They believe 'once saved always saved' meaning its ok to sin now and ask for forgiveness later. This is not how you gain access to the Kingdom of Heaven.

- The government attempts to control churches by telling them what they can and cannot mention behind the pulpit.
- California is promoting a bill that would ban advertising or engaging in sexual orientation change efforts. It will become illegal for Christians to speak the truth and minister about homosexuality and gender changes with this bill.
- Christians are harassed about their Biblical beliefs. They are called bigots and haters. This has left Christians afraid to witness, to speak out about what they believe and it has even led strong Christian believers astray.

The question is, which persecution is more dangerous? It's agreed that physical torture and abuse is not something we want nor does it give us a warm fuzzy feeling.

Physical torture is what we fear and what we pray against. Jesus warned us in Matthew 10:28

"Do not fear those who kill the body but are not able to kill the soul. But rather fear Him who is able to destroy both soul and body in hell."

The most dangerous persecution is the one that kills both your body and soul. Christian perspective is changing. Conviction is diminishing. Righteous living has become a fad. Dedication to "self" has become a priority over our dedication to Christ. With that thought in mind, let's look at the persecuted church of Smyrna.

REVELATION OF JESUS

"To the angel of the church in Smyrna write, 'These things says the First and the Last, who was dead, and came to life:' Rev. 2:8 NKJV

Jesus existed before the heavens and the earth were created. Jesus is the sacrificial lamb, the last sacrifice for sinners. Jesus died for our transgressions, conquered death and is alive and well, sitting at the right hand of the Father. Jesus always was and always will be.

COMMENDATION

"I know your works, tribulation and poverty (but you are rich)." Rev. 2:9a NKJV

Jesus knows the tribulation the church has and will suffer. Christians in Smyrna were not only physically persecuted and put to death, they were also severely impoverished. No matter how little you have, in a materialistic sense, if you are saved and walking in God's will, you ARE rich. Remember that the things of this world will surely pass away. You are only a temporary traveler on this Earth and your journey ends in Heaven. Keep moving forward and don't become discouraged because you are working towards the prize – the everlasting Kingdom of Heaven.

THE CHARGE

"and I know the blasphemy of those who say they are Jews, and are not, but are a synagogue of Satan." Rev. 2:9b NKJV

Notice how there isn't a charge against the true church of Smyrna, the ones who are persecuted? Jesus knew they were being persecuted for His name's sake.

"The Lord is near to the brokenhearted and saves the contrite of spirit. Many are the afflictions of the righteous, but the Lord delivers him out of them all." Psalms 34:18–19 MEV

Jesus has compassion for people's trials but He also knows the truth in everyone's heart. He knows the people who claim to be Christians and churches that claim to be of God but are, in reality, of Satan. They are full of deception and lies. Jesus uses the word "blasphemy" which means "an act of cursing or reviling God."

Always be in God's word so you can discern the schemes of the devil. Don't be a victim of Satan's silent persecution towards the true church of Christ.

ACTION NEEDED

"Do not fear any of those things which you are about to suffer." Rev. 2:10a NKJV

Fear is not of God. Although human flesh wants to fear the afflictions we face, Jesus encourages us not to fear.

Joseph was rejected by his brothers, but God saved him and used him for His Glory.

Moses was scared to be the one to confront Pharaoh and ask for the release of the Israelites. God showed His powerful glory and humiliated Pharaoh in the process. The Israelites simply walked away from their slavery.

David didn't hesitate to fight Goliath and God was with him in victory.

Esther knew it was up to her to save the Jews but she relied on her people to fast and pray. God granted her grace in the eyes of the king. Not only was she able to save her people, the person responsible for their annihilation was swiftly brought to justice.

Daniel and the lions; what could be scarier? It's possible that there wasn't any light in the room which left Daniel to sit in darkness. He probably heard the rumbles of the lions' roars and felt the hotness of their breath. God was faithful and shut the mouths of the lions and Daniel was set free.

How many times did the Apostle Paul face trials, tribulation and possible death? Jesus had a job for him to do and no matter the circumstance, Paul ran the race of righteousness and God was glorified in the process.

The Bible is full of examples of God's grace, mercy, and protection for those who are faithful. Regardless of the outcome, we need to have faith and know that God is with us and He has a plan.

WARNING

"Indeed, the devil is about to throw some of you into prison, that you may be tested, and you will have tribulation ten days." Rev. 2:10b NKJV

Don't worry and seclude yourself from society based on this passage. We were told to occupy until Jesus returns and remember, fear is not of God. Many Christians during the persecution of Smyrna were judged, imprisoned, tortured and put to death. We also know, based on the scriptures, the world hates those who follow Jesus. So, persecution will always be a byproduct of our faithfulness.

The Hebrew meaning of "ten" represents a complete congregation, body, or kingdom, whether good or evil.[1]

We know, based on the scriptures, there will be times of trouble for the church of Christ — The Hebrew meaning of "days" changes, based on the context and wording. It could mean a literal day (24 hours), a season, a period of time or a year.[2]

This is by no means a prediction of when Jesus will return or how long persecution will last. History tells us there have been many kings and kingdoms since the church of Smyrna that reigned terror on the followers of Christ. It's certain there will be more evil kingdoms to come if Christ's return is delayed.

ENCOURAGEMENT FOR THE OVERCOMER

"Be faithful until death, and I will give you the crown of life. "He who has an ear, let him hear what the Spirit says to the churches. He who overcomes shall not be hurt by the second death." Revelation 2:10c-11 NKJV

There are five crowns mentioned in the New Testament for the believers that have persevered:

1. The Imperishable Crown – a reward given to those who have faithfully endured. This crown will not fade away unlike the things of earth. This crown is undefiled and incorruptible. (1 Corinthians 9:24–25)

2. The Crown of Rejoicing – we are told to rejoice always in the Lord. As Christians we have a hope and joy that the world cannot understand. Even during our trials and tribulations we are encouraged and joyful. God promises us that when we go to heaven there will be no more tears, no death or sorrow. (Revelation 21:4)

3. The Crown of Righteousness–this is not of our own righteousness, it is the righteousness of Christ that we have inherited through our salvation and faithfulness. We have rightfully obtained this crown, it was not granted through deceit or compromise. It is a crown of eternity to those that love the Lord and eagerly await his return. (2 Timothy 4:8)

4. The Crown of Glory – glory is the very nature of God. It is who he is and it is his actions. Because of our love and faithfulness we are able to wear His glory, His splendor and brightness! Our praise and honor are to God and God alone and we are blessed to be allowed in His kingdom. (1 Peter 5:4)

5. The Crown of Life – all believers that love God and follow His commandments will receive the crown of life. There is something more meaningful for those that have endured persecution and prevailed. The crown of life indicates our bravery, our eternity, our perseverance and dedication to Jesus. Best of all, it's for eternity!

Regardless of the persecution you may endure, know that God is with you, God loves you and you are strong through God.

"Therefore, since we are encompassed with such a great cloud of witnesses, let us also lay aside every weight and the sin that so easily entangles us, and let us run with endurance the race that is set before us. Let us look to Jesus, the author and finisher of our faith, who for the joy that was set before Him endured the cross, despising the shame, and is seated at the right hand of the throne of God. For consider Him who endured such hostility from sinners against Himself, lest you become weary and your hearts give up." Hebrews 12:1–3 MEV

Endnotes:
1. https://graceintorah.net/2015/06/15/hebrew-numbers-1–10/
2. https://www.ancient-hebrew.org/definition/

DAY ONE - PRAYER FOCUS

Repent for glorifying your trials and tribulations instead of having faith in God and highlighting His blessings.

Ask the Lord to give you peace within your circumstance. Ask to know that your situation can never be compared to what others have endured. Ask the Lord to show you that He is with you no matter what.

Scripture References:
Psalms 34:1–3
Philippians 4:12–13
1 Peter 1:6

DAY TWO - PRAYER FOCUS

Repent for allowing tribulations to weigh you down and give you a sense of defeat.

Ask the Lord to increase your desire for more of him in the midst of trials and tribulations. Ask the Lord to reveal himself even more to you during these troubled times.

Scripture References:
John 14:27
1 Peter 4:12–13
2 Corinthians 1:3–4

DAY THREE - PRAYER FOCUS

Repent for allowing other people's hatred towards Christian values fill you with unrighteous anger.

Ask God to help you forgive those that persecute you and to earnestly pray for them to gain Godly wisdom and understanding.

Pray for God to reveal himself to these people so that God is glorified.

Scripture References:
Ephesians 4:31–32
Proverbs 10:12
Luke 6:27–28

DAY FOUR - PRAYER FOCUS

Repent for not recognizing your wealth in Christ and complaining about what you don't have.
Ask the Lord to give you a new vision of what wealth is, to renew your mind and set your heart on His promise.

Scripture References:
Matthew 6:20–21
1 Timothy 6:18–19
Colossians 3:1–3

DAY FIVE - PRAYER FOCUS

Repent for not relying on the Holy Spirit to give you the words and wisdom for either yourself or others in the midst of persecution.
Ask the Lord to fill your heart and mouth with words of encouragement. Pray for those that cannot recognize God's presence within the persecution.

Scripture References:
Joshua 1:9
Psalms 73:25–26
Psalms 143:11

DAY SIX - PRAYER FOCUS

Repent for not speaking truth and fearing what others may think of you.

Ask the Lord to give you strength when someone speaks ill of Jesus or Christianity. Ask the Lord to give you words of wisdom to combat those that twist what the Lord's word truly says. Ask for strength to speak in love when others make fun of biblical morals and views.

Scripture References:
Proverbs 12:18
1 Peter 3:15–16
Jude 1:3–4

DAY SEVEN - PRAYER FOCUS

Repent for tainting your witness of Christ and testimony with complaints and constant reminders of what you endured.

Ask God to use your misery for his ministry without glorifying evil. Ask God to show you purpose and ways to use your talents for those in need or those being persecuted.

Scripture References:
1 Peter 2:1–2
James 1:17–18
Isaiah 5:20

Chapter Four

A Clean House is a Happy Home

..."a house divided against a house falls."
Luke 11:17 NKJVb

A person would most likely encounter the wilderness as they traveled from city to city in Biblical times.

The wilderness is classified as an uncultivated place such as the desert or a field. There was a scattered group of people who lived in the wilderness. These people had a meager existence, residing in secluded shanties either alone or in a small group.

They were outcasts; dead to society and forbidden to come within six feet of another Israelite. You could hear them shout "Tamei! Tamei!" if you dared to venture near. Tamei was a warning, a sounding alarm of impending contamination if you came dangerously close to their proximity.

These were the Lepers of Biblical times. They were commanded to separate themselves from society according to the law (Lev. 13:45–46). When a person had a sore or rash on their skin, they were commanded to show the priest. The priest would examine the person and determine whether the skin condition was leprous. The priest would declare a person who had positive signs of leprosy as unclean.

Not everyone declared unclean had leprosy as we know it today. Leprosy was a word used for numerous skin conditions such as psoriasis or any infectious rash. A process was put in place for temporary skin conditions so they could be declared clean once it healed and showed no signs of spreading.

Leprosy (Hansen's disease as it's called today) is a chronic infectious disease. This disease affects the nerves, skin, upper respiratory tract, eyes, and lining of the nose. There was no cure for leprosy in biblical times which is why an affected person was declared dead to society and forbidden to come close to any Israelite or cultivated area.

An infectious disease starts as an infection which is when harmful bacteria or a virus enters the body and attacks the cells. God provided us with an immune system capable of fighting against contamination but when we don't take care of our body or if we have a genetic condition; our immune system can become compromised.

With a compromised immune system, the bacteria or virus can damage the cells; this damage is called disease.

Some diseases are curable, while others are incurable (outside of God's divine healing and mercy). Up until the 20th century, there was no cure for leprosy. Your version of the Bible most likely states a leprous person had to cry "unclean" when they were in close proximity of another person. In our modern day, we characterize unclean to mean dirty, unkempt, sick or disgusting. The Hebrew word used for unclean was tamei which has a much deeper meaning.

Tamei or Tameh means impurity. This may seem like a word we would clearly associate with unclean, but the Hebrew word goes much deeper than impure. Tameh comes from the root word, "satum," which means closed off and signifies a disconnection from life; there is no possibility for growth or movement—it is dead.

There was a church remnant that compromised the teachings of God's word. This was true when Revelation was written and is certainly true with many churches today.

Compromise begins with an infection. A person or persons deviate from God's will and standards. Their concessions and accommodations do not line up with the whole word of God.

God gave us an immune system (The Armor of God — Ephesians 6:11–18) that is designed to fight off and expose the enemy's attempts to infect the Church.

We are told to stand firm and surround ourselves with truth, to have a righteous heart, to cover our steps with the gospel of peace, to use the protection of faith to ward off evil attacks, to keep our salvation close to mind using the word of God as our guide and to PRAY. Our watchfulness will help us persevere.

If we don't use what God gave us, our protection against the enemy is compromised. A church that yields to or permits this infection, transmits untruth and damages the congregation. The church is now riddled with disease; it is unclean, impure – it is tameh.

How can you recognize a person or church with a strong immune system?

1. They seek to bring the glory of God to all areas of their life. Worldly desires fade away.

2. Fear subsides as their trust in Christ increases. Fear of circumstances, fear of the future and fear of death, is replaced by rejoicing in the Lord.

3. Their identity is hidden in Christ. They no longer seek the approval of man, nor do they need to compare themselves to others.

4. They are not taken by surprise when trials come their way; it's expected. They are confident, knowing that Christ walks with them and in the end, God will be glorified.

How can you recognize a person or church that has been compromised?

1. Worldly desires overtake the desire to please God. God's glory is no longer what's sought after; pleasure takes precedence.

2. Fear is just a way of life because they feel the world is a fearful place. There's no faith in Christ being in the midst. There is fear of circumstance, fear of the future and fear of death. Godly fear and reverence have been lost.

3. A person's (or church's) identity is based upon the opinion of others. They tend to compare themselves to others and live in a manner so they will not be judged by man.

4. Life's trials become an offense, especially when they are taught all Christians should live in peace and prosperity. They wonder why it always happens to them, when will they live a peaceful life and what have they done wrong?

COMPROMISE IS A SLOW FADE

A compromising church doesn't intend to compromise God's word. Unfortunately, some churches think they've been immobilized (unmoved) by sitting on a solid foundation. So they relocate their church into an RV (religious venue) thinking it will be more beneficial to 'The Way'. Churches begin to experiment.

Maybe attendance is low, and they want to try new things to reach the lost, but in the process, they themselves become lost.

Maybe the community thinks the church is too 'rigid' so they begin to adopt worldly views so people will come.

Maybe people left their church to go to the new and upcoming one down the road, so the church begins to adopt some of the same programs and concepts just to compete.

Maybe a new minister wants to spice up the congregation, so they introduce ungodly beliefs. They misquote scripture to justify the new beliefs and the unwise congregation plays follow-the-leader.

Whatever the case, compromise is unrighteous and very dangerous. The once church of God unknowingly becomes a church of Satan.   Let's see what Jesus thought of the church in Pergamos.

REVELATION OF JESUS

"And to the angel of the church in Pergamos write, 'These things says He who has the sharp two-edged sword:" Rev. 2:12 NKJV

Jesus is the One Who holds the Word of God; Jesus IS the Word of God (John 1:1). Just as Jesus used God's Word to deal with Satan, He will use it to deal with the compromiser. God's Word can create or destroy, heal or afflict, soothe or trouble.

The result depends upon which image they are willing to become. Will it be the image of Christ (Truth) or the image of man (compromise)?

Jesus used the Word of God to correct unsound doctrine and practices. Jesus rebuked Satan in the desert by quoting God's law written in Deuteronomy.

Jesus publicly rebuked and corrected the Pharisees and Sadducees by using God's Word. This was done so all could hear the dangers of their false doctrines and misinterpretations.

The phrase Jesus most commonly used was "You have heard it said [. . .] but I say to you." Jesus also used the phrase "Have you not heard it said…" or "It is written" when referencing Old Testament doctrine. Jesus quoted from 24 different Old Testament books during His ministry on earth. The purpose of these quotes was to confirm, teach, rebuke and correct.

COMMENDATION

"I know your works, and where you dwell, where Satan's throne is. And you hold fast to My name and did not deny My faith even in the days in which Antipas was My faithful martyr, who was killed among you, where Satan dwells." Rev. 2:13 NKJV

Jesus knew about the city of Pergamos, an area that merged church and state. (Does that sound a little familiar?). Intellectual heathens governed the city, therefore it was given over to idolatry.

Some of the temples of worship in Pergamos included:

1. Athena – she is depicted as leading soldiers into battle.

2. Caesar Augustus – he was depicted as the son of god or the eternal Caesar. He was publicly adored, and oaths were taken on the divine spirit of the emperor.

3. Dionysus – was deemed as a god who had the power to inspire and create ecstasy.

4. Asklepios – was deemed a god of medicine and healing.

5. Hadrian – was an emperor with a young male lover. After his lover's death, Hadrian stated his lover conquered death and became a god for his self-sacrifice.

6. Zeus – was a mythical creature believed to be the god of the sky and weather. They would offer sacrifices, thinking he would bring them rain.

Satan's power was strong in Pergamos, but the power of the Holy Spirit was stronger because Christians refused to surrender. They didn't back down from their beliefs just like Antipas, whose faithfulness was worthy of being mentioned by Jesus himself directly from the throne of God.

When we look at the reasons people worshipped these gods, we can clearly see our world as it is today. People are idolized for being great leaders, generals, and outstanding individuals. People search for worldly desires such as inspiration, ecstasy, medicine and healing. Same-sex relationships have been glorified within society. Governments are trying to find ways to control the weather.

There is no doubt that Satan is at work and his power is strong in this world. We must remember - OUR God is stronger!

THE CHARGE

"But I have a few things against you, because you have those who hold the doctrine of Balaam, who taught Balak to put a stumbling block before the children of Israel, to eat things sacrificed to idols, and to commit sexual immorality. Thus, you also have those who hold the doctrine of the Nicolaitans, which thing I hate." Rev. 2:14–15 NKJV

In the midst of Pergamos' evil, the church allowed those with the spirit of Balaam and the Nicolaitans to not only attend their services but to infiltrate the congregation with their beliefs and customs.

DOCTRINE OF BALAAM

Balaam is a diviner in the Torah whose story begins in Chapter 22 of the Book of Numbers. Followers of Balaam had no qualms about deceiving, conniving, seducing, and sinning. They enticed others to follow suit. Sexual immorality and idolism were just a way of living to them. Violence, rape, murder, and injustice were in the daily reports.

The patriarch, Moses, laid down clear instructions to separate from the pagan style of living and worshipping, "Break down their altars and smash their sacred pillars. Burn their Asherah poles and cut down their carved idols. Completely erase the names of their gods! Do not worship the LORD your God in the way these pagan peoples worship their gods." (Deuteronomy 12:3-4)

Gideon became the first to fight against the infestation of Asherah poles, although, in his fear, he chopped down his father's Asherah pole at night (Judges 6:25-27). Isn't it the most difficult thing to risk the favor and peaceful relationship of your parent, sibling, or child? Don't give up!

The books of 1 & 2 Kings and 1 & 2 Chronicles tell a long story of one king chopping down Asherah poles and another building them back up.

Then, during the days of the kings of Israel, the Bible says Asa did what was good and right in the eyes of the LORD his God. (Going against the policies of all the other kings, and beyond what was socially acceptable for the people of Israel), he removed the foreign altars and the high places, smashed the sacred stones and cut down the Asherah poles. He commanded Judah to seek the LORD, the God of their ancestors, and to obey His laws and commands.

"He removed the high places and incense altars in every town in Judah, and the kingdom was at peace under him.

"He built up the fortified cities of Judah [...] no-one was at war with him during those years for the Lord gave him rest."

Following Balaam offers sexual immorality, idols, and violence as a lifestyle and for entertainment.

The Lord, offers peace, security, rest, and prosperity.

When a foreign king, Zerah the Cushite, marched out against Judah with chariots and thousands upon thousands of troops, Asa met him with his well-fortified army of brave fighting men. But, this is not what saved Judah. Before the battles started, "Asa called to the LORD, 'LORD, there is no one like you to help the powerless against the mighty. Help us, Lord our God, for we rely on you, and in your name, we have come against this vast army. LORD, you are our God; do not let mere mortals prevail against you.'"

"The LORD struck down the Cushites [. . .] such a great number of Cushites fell that they could not recover; they were crushed before the LORD and his forces. The men carried off a large amount of plunder."

The Lord offers the plunder when we honor Him. He conquers our enemies and gives us the spoils. 2 Chronicles 14:2–15 NLB

"The Spirit of God came on Azariah son of Oded. He went out to meet Asa and said to him, 'Listen to me, Asa and all Judah and Benjamin. The LORD is with you when you are with him. If you seek him, he will be found by you, but if you forsake him, he will forsake you. For a long time, Israel was without the true God, without a priest to teach and without the law. But in their distress, they turned to the LORD, the God of Israel, and sought him, and he was found by them. In those days it was not safe to travel about, for all the inhabitants of the lands were in great turmoil. One nation was being crushed by another and one city by another, because God was troubling them with every kind of distress. But as for you, be strong and do not give up, for your work will be rewarded.'

"When Asa heard these words of the prophecy, he took courage. He removed the detestable idols from the whole land. [...] They repaired the altar of the LORD [...] They assembled [...] They entered into a covenant to seek the LORD, the God of their ancestors, with all their heart and soul." 2 Chronicles 15:1–12.

Whom will you serve?

DOCTRINE OF NICOLAITANS

There are many beliefs about this doctrine, making it complicated to pinpoint the exact meaning of Jesus' statement. One theory that seems to fit is the Nicolaitans felt the soul is generally good, while the flesh is evil.

With this belief in mind, the Nicolaitans concluded it didn't matter what they did with/in the flesh because it wouldn't affect their spirit. Therefore, the Nicolaitans lived it up and did whatever the flesh desired because immorality wasn't a factor.

Sound familiar in our modern world?

There is a belief in the Church today that God will save everyone, no matter what.

God is not deceived. He knows the heart. He knows the intent of someone's action or words.

One version of this doctrine essentially says, after someone initially confesses one's sins asking Jesus to be Lord and Savior, it doesn't matter how the person's life is lived.

Another form of this doctrine is seen in the church attendees who feel they will receive their heavenly wings simply by attending church and tithing on a regular basis.

Yet another misnomer of grace teaches salvation comes from membership or baptism in a particular church, then a parishioner can live however he or she chooses during the week so long as the knee is bent before the confessional at the end.

There are a variety of misbeliefs. Some believe that God is so good and loving that our attitude toward Him doesn't matter at all.

Certain non-believers (as well as certain religions) believe they are inherently good because they do good things, or at least they don't do worse things than the next person; therefore, they will go to heaven because who can blame them personally for a culture of sin?

No-matter-what is the Nicolaitan's philosophy. Passage to heaven is guaranteed, paved by the good intentions of a loving God, is their philosophy.

You can almost hear Jesus say, "Whoa, to you who believe anything other than God is holy and humanity is fallen. Only my supreme sacrifice in laying down my life to buy your peace with the Father has that kind of reconciliation power! If you don't care for me here in your life on earth, if you never turn to me in trust for help, if you do not allow me to lead and guide you as your Lord God, then why would you want to dwell in eternity with me — or I with you?"

True faith has fruit. Staying in the true vine you can watch the evidence of your salvation begin to bud and fruit in your relationships and in your thirst for more of the Lord.

The intent of one's repentance and conversion cannot be pitted with fraud or deception at the core.

God's word clearly tells us that we can fall from grace (Gal. 5:1–5), be led away by wickedness (2 Peter 3:17), wander from the truth (James 5:19–20) and willfully walk away from God (Heb. 3:12). So, recognizing His word speaks with authority when it tells us that all have sinned and fallen short of the Glory of God (Rom. 3:23), then we are able to rest from any doubts about Christ's work being efficient, and we can also rest from continuing our own work thinking that somehow good deeds can bring us to glory.

The wheels of our good deed are always too flat and there is not enough gas, nor do good deeds have wings. Good deeds don't save us (Eph. 2:8–9). Salvation comes only through the saving grace of Jesus Christ and the blood He shed on the cross. That visit to hell was made in substitution for us paying our own penalty for offending God. He separates us from our sin at our point of repentance because Holy God cannot look on sin. Christ carried our sins to hell. Sin is felled, and we are raised up to friendship, freedom and righteousness and to eternal life in Christ.

The church does not have the authority to decide what is good and what is evil, what is right and what is wrong. Only the Word of God, inspired by the Holy Spirit, has the authority to do that.

Christians are to honor the God of their ancestors like Asa King of Judah and the Benjamites did. Christians are examples of Jesus Christ, set apart from the ways of the world. We don't capitulate to pressure, manipulation, or enticements to lower ourselves. We refrain from acting out as the world does. We are to be the light within the darkness. If the church operates in a fog, how can Christ's glory and transforming love ever be known?

Ask God to help you understand. Walk with Him. Talk with Him. Meditate on His truth.

a) We receive salvation by sincerely believing in Jesus' work (John 3:16–17).
b) Although we are encouraged to fellowship with one another (Heb. 10:25), going to church won't save us.
c) No one goes to heaven without making Jesus their Lord and Savior (John 14:6).

ACTION NEEDED

"Repent, or else I will come to you quickly and will fight against them with the sword of My mouth." Rev. 2:16 NKJV

Jesus tells the compromising church to repent or else He will quickly use the Word of God to fight against their evil ways and it won't be pleasant.

The Word will:

- Reveal all things that pertain to godliness (1 Peter 1:3)
- Shine the light of God and expose sin (John 3:20)
- Convict people of sin (John 8:7)
- Reveal the love of God (John 3:16)
- Reveal God's judgments (Romans 14:10)
- Call for people to repent (Acts 2:38)

ENCOURAGEMENT FOR THE OVERCOMER

"He who has an ear, let him hear what the Spirit says to the churches. To him who overcomes I will give some of the hidden manna to eat. And I will give him a white stone, and on the stone a new name written which no one knows except him who receives it." Rev. 2:17 NKJV

God fed the Israelites with a heavenly manna while they wandered in the wilderness. This manna fed them when there was a shortage of food.

Jesus is the hidden manna that will spiritually feed us.
We will never thirst or hunger in Christ Jesus.

There are many interpretations as to the meaning of the white stone mentioned after the manna. The two most likely are:

1. Stones were used to cast votes within the justice system; black for guilty and white for innocent. Jesus is telling us that if we allow him into our life and follow His laws without compromise, we will be found innocent in the Court of the Most High. Our sins will be blotted out.

2. In ancient times a white stone was awarded to the victors of athletic games. This white stone allowed them to attend a special award banquet. Jesus is giving a promise to the overcomer (victor) that they will reside in heaven eternally and attend the Great Banquet.[3]

"But now, thus says the Lord who created you, O Jacob, and He who formed you, O Israel: Do not fear, for I have redeemed you; I have called you by your name; you are Mine." Isaiah 43:1 MEV

Jesus has given the redeemed a new name, a name only He knows. This name will be revealed to us as Jesus hands us our very own white stone of innocence. **"The stone that the builders rejected has become the cornerstone."** Psalms 118:22

Endnote:

3.   https://www.gotquestions.org/white-stone-new-name.html

https://www.biblestudytools.com/commentaries/revelation/revelation-2/revelation-2-17.html

DAY ONE - PRAYER FOCUS

Repent for the times you didn't set yourself apart from the world, for the times when you did as others did just so you could be part of the crowd.

Ask the Lord to give you a greater sense of pride for your salvation. Ask him to help you to not be ashamed of your Christianity around those with worldly views.

Scripture References:
Psalms 4:3
Isaiah 61:10
Exodus 23:2a

DAY TWO - PRAYER FOCUS

Repent for the times you sought mankind's approval instead of seeking God's.

Ask the Lord to help you see yourself as he sees you. Ask him to help you not look for man's approval but to have confidence in the Lord and the Lord himself.

Scripture References:
Psalms 118:8–9
Galatians 1:10
Psalms 139:17–18

DAY THREE - PRAYER FOCUS

Repent for the times you settled for the mainstream theology, when you believed an idea just because someone said so without researching it yourself.

Ask the Lord to give you a fervent Berean spirit. Ask the Lord to help you become a noble Berean by receiving the word of God with wisdom and readiness.

Scripture References:
Colossians 2:8
Hosea 6:6
Hebrews 4:12

DAY FOUR - PRAYER FOCUS

Repent for not recognizing the spiritual war of deception raging around you.

Ask the Lord to give you divine discernment so you are always aware of the forces of darkness attempting to deceive you. Pray that your conviction for Jesus will be a powerful light in this dark world.

Scripture References:
Ephesians 4:18
Hebrews 5:14
Proverbs 2:11–15

DAY FIVE - PRAYER FOCUS

Repent for the times you sacrificed God's blessings for temporary pleasures.

Ask the Lord to fill your heart with a desire for his blessings above worldly pleasures.

Scripture References:
1 Timothy 5:6
Isaiah 44:3
Proverbs 10:22

DAY SIX - PRAYER FOCUS

Repent for not recognizing where our life, the lives of our family, the life of our church and the lives of our community have gone astray.

Pray for the strength to reprove those who have gone astray in a Biblical manner and that God will open their hearts to hear what the Holy Spirit has to say. Pray that God will show you the plank in your own eye so you can repent.

Scripture References:
Ezekiel 3:21
1 John 1:10
1 John 3:10

DAY SEVEN - PRAYER FOCUS

Repent for not reaching out to those who have been deceived by compromise. Repent for not having compassion on those bound for hell.

Ask the Lord to help you reach those who are lost. Ask for guidance to witness to those who have been deceived. Ask for God to reveal the truth to those with whom you speak.

Scripture References:
Mark 16:15–16
Acts 1:8
2 Timothy 1:8–12

Chapter Five

Expose the Evil

**"You have set our iniquities before You,
even our secret sins in the light of Your presence"**
Psalms 90:8 MEV

A young newlywed, wanting to please her husband, decided to cook him a roast for dinner because she was taught, 'the way to a man's heart is through his stomach.'

Her Momma was one of the best cooks she knew so she decided the best course of action was to duplicate Momma's recipe. She searched until she found the perfect roast. She picked out only fresh herbs and chopped fresh vegetables. Once everything was prepared, she cut the roast in half. One half of the roast was braised, placed in a pan with the other ingredients and then placed into the oven. The other half of the roast was placed in the refrigerator.

Her husband was impressed with the impeccable meal from his new bride. The meat was tender, the carrots savory, the gravy flavorful, and the potatoes *just right*.

He complimented her on such a lovely meal, but curiosity got the best of him. He asked his wife, "That was such a wonderful meal but I'm curious as to why you cooked half of the roast and placed the other half in the fridge." She thought for a moment and responded, "That's the way Momma used to do it." The husband, still in a savory coma, accepted her theory. But the wife couldn't stop thinking about it.

"Why did Momma make her roast that way?" she pondered. The next day she decided to call her Mom and ask. "Momma, I was wondering why you cut your roast in half and only cooked a portion of it?" There was a brief silence on the phone as her Mother pondered the question. Finally, she answered, "I'm not sure. I guess it's because that's how your Grandma always cooked the roast."

The wife was content to know that she was following family tradition. Grandma was an even better cook than her Momma, so she must be on the right track. Although the wife was content, Mom's curiosity got the best of her. "Why did Grandma cook her roast that way?" she pondered.

The next day Mom called Grandma and asked "I was wondering something. When you cooked a roast for the family you cut it in half and only cooked one half while you placed the other half in the fridge. Why did you do that?"

Without hesitation, Grandma replied, "That's easy. We had a very small oven."

We all have family traditions. Whether it's how we celebrate holidays or special events, how we raise our families or simple recipes we prepare, family traditions are meant to be cherished and passed on to upcoming generations.

There are religions that have incorporated traditions and doctrines that people still follow to this day. Some of these doctrines are outright evil, and an abomination to God, yet these religions are thriving and souls are being lost daily.

Jesus wants them to repent; He wants them to know the truth. Everyone will be judged for their acceptable and unacceptable behavior and actions. Are you following what's right? Are you prepared? Is Jesus your ally? Have you repented for the unacceptable?

REVELATION OF JESUS

"And to the angel of the church in Thyatira write, 'These things says the Son of God, who has eyes like a flame of fire, and His feet are like fine brass:" Rev. 2:18 NKJV

This statement clarifies the deity of Jesus, that He is truly the Son of God. He is not just the God of men, He is the God of the Universe, the God of creation…He is THE one and ONLY God.

Jesus sees all, He is omniscient. Jesus has complete, and unlimited knowledge, awareness and understanding of every church's conduct(s). He also has complete and unlimited knowledge, awareness and understanding of each individual's action and heart. In other words, Jesus knows you better than you know yourself.

Jesus will judge with perfect wisdom. Jesus will act with strength and He will be steadfast in His judgment.

COMMENDATION

"I know your works, love, service, faith, and your patience, and as for your works, the last are more than the first." Rev. 2:19 NKJV

Jesus acknowledges not one, but six individual characteristics of the church in Thyatira.

1. Works: Their righteous actions were products of their good deeds and works. He was not referring to works done for human satisfaction, Jesus was talking about the good deeds they did to glorify the Father in Heaven. Matthew 5:16

2. Love: When working in the will of God you will naturally do so with a charitable, loving heart. They loved the Lord their

God and that love was shown to mankind throughout their ministry. Hebrews 6:10

3. Service: They exercised their good works in love producing a service (or ministry) to not only the church but also to the community. This could mean teaching and ministering within the church or reaching out to those in need throughout the community. Galatians 6:2

4. Faith: They had faith in salvation through our Lord Jesus Christ. They worked within that faith, producing ministries of love. John 16:33

5. Patience: They endured with patience. Living amongst evil can make one anxious, but they were patient in the Lord. The fruit of their love and faith in Christ produced patience. Revelation 14:12

Last works are more than the first: Every Christian should strive to become better in all that they do for the Lord. This progression comes by staying strong, desiring to know God more every day, studying His Word daily, endurance through prayer and worship and righteously exercising that which has been learned. This church didn't stop after the first, second or third ministry, they continued to grow.

The ministries didn't grow in just numbers but also in creditability. Proverbs 4:18

THE CHARGE

"Nevertheless, I have a few things against you, because you allow that woman Jezebel, who calls herself a prophetess, to teach and seduce My servants to commit sexual immorality and eat things sacrificed to idols. And I gave her time to repent of her sexual immorality, and she did not repent." Rev. 2:20–21 NKJV

Queen Jezebel first appeared in 1 Kings chapter 16. She married King Ahab and brought pure evilness into Israel. She came from a kingdom marinated in Baal worship; therefore, she used her sexuality to manipulate, dominate, seduce and destroy anyone who crossed her path.

Although God brought judgment upon the queen, the Jezebel spirit is alive and well within our society and the church today. It's important to know the attributes of the Jezebel Spirit so that the true church of Christ can identify this spirit quickly before it has the chance to infiltrate the congregation.

This cunning and intelligent spirit wants nothing more than to secretly and seductively destroy anyone and anything related to God. The best line of defense is education so you can recognize the spirit and pray against it.

Before we continue, let's make one thing clear; a true born-again Christian cannot be possessed by an evil spirit/demon. Our bodies are temples of the Holy Spirit. But don't get too relaxed. A true born-again Christian is not immune to the influence of evil spirits to be captivated by sin or captured in physical or psychological prisons by others' sin.

• Demonic influence is when an evil spirit tries to influence the emotions and will of a person, causing them to be led away from the safety of the Lord and the support of His community. During this time, the person maintains control over their actions. A person can overcome temptation to sin with confession, prayer, good counsel, healthy distractions, and other Biblical disciplines.

• Demonic possession happens when a person who is not filled with the Holy Spirit opens himself up and allows evil spirits to take control over his or her reasoning, human feelings, actions and will. A person can be delivered from demonic possession.

WARNING

Satan's ultimate goal is to drive a wedge so far in-between you and God that you walk away from your salvation. With that said, a person who continually gives in to evil spiritual influences opens himself up for more attacks from the enemy. A person who continues to give in to evil influences and refuses to ask for forgiveness, can walk away from their salvation and be considered a person who has rebelled against God. When a person has rebelled against God, the indwelling spirit of God is removed, making that person more vulnerable to demonic possession.

Identifying a Jezebel Spirit: (NOTE: although some context has a feminine connotation, the Jezebel Spirit can be inhabited by a male or a female)

1. Manipulation – this spirit is a master of manipulation. It secretly works behind the scenes to deceive people into believing ungodly lies or practices. This tactic is also used to cause dissension between the congregation, friendships, leadership and ultimately the truth in God's word. These spirits are cunning yet charismatic. Their alluring personality is attractive and easily entices innocent people to follow their lead, eventually leading them down the path of destruction. Some of the traits you might see within the church are:

   a. Gossiping
   b. Slandering
   c. Criticism
   d. Complaining
   e. Use of self-pity and highlighting their own weaknesses to get their way

2. Master man-hater – this spirit truly hates men and especially those in leadership. It may not be evident in the

beginning, but as this spirit begins to manifest itself, its true motive will be exposed. Some of the traits you might see within the church or families are:

a. Feminism – the feeling that women are always mistreated by men or the feeling that women are considered second-class citizens. Since this is perceived as truth, they immediately go to this premise as the fault for every problem, and they seek to vindicate "being feminine" on all accounts.

b. They feel they have to make a stand for womanhood, sexuality, and feminine leadership, with an aim of gaining more influence or authority even when a particular sphere of authority is not within the female's wheelhouse.

c. Jumping to conclusions and making statements such as, "Only men are given leadership roles" or "Men are the only ones allowed to pray" and "Only men are called upon," are some examples you may see.

d. Constant broken relationships with men.

e. Emasculating men – putting men down in front of others, making fun of being male. Constant control of men – they tell the man what to say, do, feel and what to wear.

3. Unsubmissive –The Jezebel spirit sees itself as the goddess of its own pedestal and despises anyone in authority. Once again, it may not be evident in the beginning, but their actions will eventually expose their true motive. Some of the traits you might see within the church or families are:

a. Attempting to overthrow the spiritual head of the household through manipulation or sabotage.

b. Being disrespectful to those in leadership for human weaknesses – either in front of others, or behind their backs rather than praying for the Lord's intervention and making healthier inner personal decisions.

c. Deliberately not taking godly direction from those in leadership, writing off their advice as being offensive or unnecessary.

d. Assuming the role of a leader for the purpose of undermining the leader's position and authority. They answer questions, complete tasks, make decisions, assign tasks and give directions without a leader's permission or knowledge. This gives the perception that they are in charge and undermines leadership.

e. They act as if they are above the rules/regulations.

f. They react in anger and become defensive with constructive criticism.

4. Controlling –The main objective of the Jezebel spirit is to obtain complete control, and they will do anything to gain it. Those with the Jezebel spirit appear as super achievers, highly intelligent and gifted with many talents. These traits initially make them popular and well-liked among the congregation members who are blinded to the rotten fruit being produced. Remember, you will know a spirit by its fruits and by discernment from the Holy Spirit when things begin to spiral into confusion. We have to discern the difference between a personality in a position of influence and someone who is producing genuine, good fruit. Some of the Jezebel traits you might see within the church are:

a. They have a bossy nature about them, but they become offended when their own authority is questioned.

b. They have a persona of being superior to others. They have experienced everything others have experienced. Their tribulations were greater than other people's tribulations. They glorify themselves instead of God's work and His many kindnesses. Essentially, they accept the worship of others and expect to receive no critique of person or work, only accolades. They've done it all, seen it all, experienced it all and know it all and they have no problem voicing their superiority.

c. They want to be involved in every physical or spiritual benefit available, and it is this goal that motivates them, not actually pleasing the Lord.

d. In public, they are very different to what they are in private. They flaunt themselves and strive to be noticed by all, but privately, they are mean, demeaning, punishing, and withholding of love or protection to those closest to them. They can be cruel to others who appear to be of no consequence. They use people as objects to get what they want.

e. Although many households feature a dominate person, these people dominate family members in unChrist-like ways. They have unrealistic expectations of others.

f. Not understanding the importance of others' giftedness or God's purpose in respecting others' sphere of influence, they seek to lead in as many projects and ministries as they can so that the work cannot go forward without them.

Regardless of whether God has gifted them for the position, or called them to it, they assume responsibilities and, in their effort, at times become bullish. NOTE: Leaders are appointed by God; He alone equips those whom he's designed for leadership roles, and He often equips people through education or life challenges or being mentored by someone who has gone before.

g. They are perfectionists and narcissists. They forget that it is God Who works and wills His purposes to be accomplished even through imperfect people. Depending on how long the spirit has manifested itself, they become bitter, angry, resentful, perverted, covetous and back-stabbing.

Sin can be separated from the sinner.

Please don't mistake the characteristics of the Jezebel spirit for the soul whom Jesus Christ died for, even when you have to deal with a person like this.

Just know that God's loving kindnesses extend to every living person. His kind disciplines aim to separate the shark-like spirit from the soul to be saved. He is in the business of renovating lives.

Pray and help those who appear to be masters of deception; self-ambitious, touchy or lustful, and possessive of others or worldly things. If they are convinced that they are right, the Bible has laid out a means of confrontation, even short separations from the church, and a means to forgiveness and reconciliation through a careful period of accountability. Our goal in Christ is never to condemn the person in sin, but to be an ambassador of God's truth in love to disciple and train them in better, godly choices, giving them a vision for finding their good purposes in life and also finding their limits, and to introduce them to healthy forms of entertainment and love.

The Bible warns us to be careful of ourselves when we are holding someone else accountable, praying for them, or helping them. You can see how dangerous this spirit is.

One thing to note: even though the church of Thyatira allowed someone with this dangerous spirit to not only teach but to seduce the congregation with ungodly beliefs, Jesus still gave her time to repent before placing judgment. Unfortunately, she didn't repent.

WARNING

"Indeed I will cast her into a sickbed, and those who commit adultery with her into great tribulation, unless they repent of their deeds. I will kill her children with death, and all the churches shall know that I am He who searches the minds and hearts. And I will give to each one of you according to your works." Rev. 2:22–23 NKJV

Jezebel is a harlot spirit – a prostitute and a whore. Where do prostitutes normally commit their crimes? In bed. Jesus promises that if they continue to play with fire and not repent, he will throw that harlot spirit and ALL of its followers into great tribulations, the fiery depths of hell.

False teachings will not be tolerated. This is why we should always test spirits and doctrines with God's word (the Bible in its entirety). If they don't hold up to the truth, then they are false teachings and should be stopped immediately.

When false teachings are allowed to continue, they become generational teachings.

Look at some of the ungodly doctrines you see in the world today (this is only a small list of false doctrines):

o Jesus is not God
o Jesus and Satan are brothers
o Jesus married and had children
o Evolution was the cause of creation
o There is no God, no heaven and no hell; we just live and then cease to exist
o Salvation is granted by grace AND works
o Baptism is necessary for salvation and/or infants must be baptized to go to heaven
o Love is properly defined however we wish
o Because God is love, that means love is God (however defined)
o God or the Holy Spirit are without physical sex or gender and therefore should be referred to in feminine genders, even though God refers to Himself as "He" in scripture
o The Holy Spirit is not God or is non-essential to life.
o Holy Spirit's intercession with groaning for us when we have no words to pray is not true today
o Mary is a part of God and is to be worshipped

- o Other religious books are on par with God's Word, and if they were written after the cannon was established, they may be more authoritative as the latter words of God
- o Emptying oneself into nature or oblivion is purification of the soul

Look at how some churches have allowed worldly living as common practice in Church membership. (Worldly Living means they believe Jesus is God, is the One Who died and rose again, but they continue to cling to their old ways of living. There is no defining difference between them and an unbeliever):

- o Couples living together before marriage
- o Encouraging desires for riches
- o Allowing people to continue to partake in addictive behaviors and/or bad habits
- o Appointing those with known besetting sins or false doctrines to lead and influence others in church activities such as communion, pastoring, counseling, or teaching.

Look at how some religions have allowed abominations and evil practices into not only their beliefs but also their teachings and leadership:

- o Worshiping or praying to Mary the mother of Jesus
- o Worshiping or praying to any other person or thing that is not the Trinity (God the Father, God the Son and the Holy Spirit)
- o Allowing homosexuals to be ministry leaders/teachers
- o Conforming to transgender ideals
- o Polygamy
- o Snake Handling
- o Grave sucking

How grievous it is to Jesus as he watches so many go astray, generation after generation. They will receive judgment according to their deeds.

Don't fall prey to the deceiving spirit of Jezebel! Continually study God's word, pray and test the teachings you hear. Test the spirits that are influencing you and others with Godly discernment.

God's love in Jesus Christ is all-sufficient and all-reaching and forbearing to each individual so long as breath is given to live. But, access to the kingdom of Heaven is not all inclusive by worldly definitions of God's love.

ACTION NEEDED

"Now to you I say, and the rest in Thyatira, as many as do not have this doctrine, who have not known the depths of Satan, as they say, I will put on you no other burden. But hold fast what you have till I come." Rev. 2:24–25 NKJV

Jesus is encouraging those that have not fallen victim to, or participated in, the evil teachings of Jezebel to continue their course until he returns or brings them home.

ENCOURAGEMENT FOR THE OVERCOMER

"And he who overcomes, and keeps My works to the end, to him I will give power over the nations – He 'shall rule them with a rod of iron; They shall be dashed to pieces like the potter's vessels' – as I also have received from My Father; and I will give him the morning star. He who has an ear, let him hear what the Spirit says to the churches." Rev. 2:26–29 NKJV

What a powerful encouragement this is to those who not only overcome but continue to hold fast to God's truth!

These are the people who do not waiver, who do not succumb to Jezebel's deception; they persist faithfully until death or until Christ's return.

In heaven they will be given a position of power; the authority to rule nations. Evil will be dashed to pieces. They will receive power and authority from Jesus just as Jesus has received power and authority from God to share in the victory and honor.

Venus was called the morning star; Jesus is called the Bright and Morning Star. The planet Venus is one of the brightest stars in the sky — as it is seen before the sun rises. This planet has been used as a navigational guide (before technology and GPS of course).

To say they will be given the morning star is to say that Jesus is giving himself as a gift to the overcomer. He promises to indwell the believer, never leave the believer and to be a bright and supreme guide during difficult times. The words sing like a blessing of a sparkling jewel in a crown, don't they?

"The people who sat in darkness have seen a great light..." Matthew 4:16a NKJV

DAY ONE - PRAYER FOCUS

Repent for the times you've allowed yourself to be influenced with a bad attitude, either towards a person or a circumstance.

Ask the Lord daily for peace that passes all understanding. Ask Him to reveal His love and grace inside of you.

Scripture References:
Philippians 2:14–15
Proverbs 17:22
John 15:9

DAY TWO - PRAYER FOCUS

Repent for the times you have disrespected the authority of leadership, either by mouth or action. Those in leadership include world leaders, government, parental figures, teachers, mentors, ministers, friends and family members. They are those in the community and in your church.

Ask the Lord to help you understand that God and God alone places leaders where they are. Pray for leaders by name. Pray that leaders will listen to Godly wisdom and are led by Godly principles. Pray for salvation for the leaders who are unsaved.

Scripture References:
Hebrews 13:17
Romans 13:1–5
Titus 3:1–2

DAY THREE - PRAYER FOCUS

Repent for the times you gossiped about, slandered or criticized someone.

Ask the Lord to help you see the beauty inside of them. If the person is unsaved, ask the Lord to continue to plant seeds of conviction and to open doors of opportunity to minister to them. Ask for a new heart, a godly vision, and a new perspective regarding the difficult people in your life.

Scripture References:
Ephesians 4:29
Proverbs16:28
Psalm 139:14
   (place the other person's name in this scripture)

DAY FOUR - PRAYER FOCUS

Repent for the times you had an unwarranted controlling nature, either towards a person or circumstance.

Ask the Lord to still your soul and help you understand that God is in control of all things. Ask the Lord to help you to know when you need to stand strong and when you need to have a humble spirit.

Scripture References:
Isaiah 14:24
Jeremiah 32:27
Psalm 55:22

DAY FIVE - PRAYER FOCUS

Repent for the times you did not notice ungodly spirits in control of a situation, or a person's actions.

Ask the Lord for a greater sense of discernment. Ask God to reveal evil intentions and spirits and that the Holy Spirit will give you the right words in which to pray against those evil spirits.

Scripture References:
1 John 4:1
1 Timothy 4:1
Ephesians 6:11

DAY SIX - PRAYER FOCUS

Identify and confess the times you have given an ear to, or succumbed to, ungodly teachings. Make a new plan.

Ask the Lord to illuminate His word to expose the lies of these ungodly teachings. Ask the Lord to reveal the truth to those who are teaching ungodly doctrine or remove them from the position of teaching for the sake of those who fall prey.

Scripture References:
Galatians 1:8–9
Romans 16:17–18
Titus 1:9–11

DAY SEVEN - PRAYER FOCUS

Lament for the deception the world has succumbed to. Lament for the numerous ungodly teachings people are being exposed to and for the souls that are lost daily because of those deceptive teachings.

Ask the Lord to give you the eyes and heart to see your grief for the condition of the world. Ask the Lord to give you wisdom and understanding to help reveal the truth to those living in deception. Ask the Lord to use you for His purpose and ministry.

Chapter Six

Keep Us Connected

"But she who lives in pleasure is dead while she lives."
1 Timothy 5:6 MEV

"But if any do not care for their own, and especially for those of their own house, they denied the faith and are worse than unbelievers."
1 Timothy 5:8 MEV

Toe bone connected to the foot bone. Foot bone connected to the heel bone. Heel bone connected to the ankle bone. Ankle bone connected to the shin bone. Shin bone connected to the knee bone. Knee bone connected to the thigh bone. Thigh bone connected to the hip bone. Hip bone connected to the back bone. Back bone connected to the shoulder bone. Shoulder bone connected to the neck bone. Neck bone connected to the head bone. Now hear the word of the Lord!

Do you remember that song? Children sang this song to understand how the skeleton connects and to help them understand the functionality of the bones in their body.

Did you know this is a Christian song? Song writer James Weldon Johnson wrote the melody, and the first recording was in 1928 by The Famous Myers Jubilee Singers.

The original name of the song was "Dem Bones" and it's based on Ezekiel 37:1–14, when God told Ezekiel to prophesy over the bones to come to life.

The beginning of the song starts at the toe bone and goes all the way to the head bone.

Christians begin at the toe bone. Salvation requires us to walk towards the cross. Our Christian walk grows the more we know God (the head). Functionality becomes limited if one bone is missing from the skeleton. If a bone is broken, the skeleton is impaired.

Just like the skeleton, the body of Christ functions from connectivity. Each 'bone' is vital to its functionality; if one part of the body is missing, its function becomes limited. If the truth is broken, the church is impaired.

The ending of the song disconnects the bones from the head down to the toe. The next letter is to Sardis. Just like some churches in today's age, Sardis was disconnected. When the church is disconnected from the headship of God, it stops walking in God's will and eventually becomes dead.

So let's hear the words of the Lord:

REVELATION OF JESUS

"And to the angel of the church in Sardis write, "These things says He who has the seven Spirits of God and the seven stars:" Rev. 3:1a NKJV

This scripture reveals not only Jesus' true nature but his authority and purpose. We will explore this revelation of Jesus more than the others because of its importance to the church of Sardis and to our walk with Christ.

Are we not called to be Christlike? Are we not supposed to be a lamp unto the world? How can we BE if we do not understand who Jesus IS?

Before we explore the Spirits of God, let's answer this question:

Why does this passage mention the 7 spirits of God?

When you understand the Hebrew meaning for the number seven it makes complete sense.

SEVEN (7) – This number is the foundation of God's word; it sums up who God is, His expectations, His purpose, and His desire for ALL. Find below, a list of words that define the meaning of the number seven (7). As you can see, the number seven speaks of the good news of Christ, how to receive salvation and how to walk in God's ways:

1. Completeness – "For in Christ lives all the fullness of God in a human body. So you also are complete through your union with Christ, who is the head over every ruler and authority." Colossians 2:9–10 (NLT)

2. Perfection – "For I will proclaim the name of the Lord: Ascribe greatness to our God! He is the Rock; His work is perfect; for all His ways are just. He is a God of faithfulness and without injustice; righteous and upright is He." Deuteronomy 32:3–4 (MEV)

3. Rest – "Come to Me, all you who labor and are heavily burdened, and I will give you rest." Matthew 11:28 (MEV)

4. Sacrifice – "I urge you therefore, brothers, by the mercies of God, that you present your bodies as a living sacrifice, holy, and acceptable to God, which is your reasonable service of worship." Romans 12:1 (MEV)

5. Purification – "Consider how much love the Father has given to us, that we should be called children of God. The world does not know us, because it did not know Him. Beloved, now are we children of God, and it has not yet been revealed what we shall be. But we know that when He appears, we shall be like Him, for we shall see Him as He is. Everyone who has this hope in Him purifies himself, just as He is pure." 1 John 3:1–3

6. Consecration – "Consecrate yourselves therefore, and be holy, for I am the Lord your God. You shall keep My statutes, and do them; I am the Lord who sanctifies you" Leviticus 20:7–8 (MEV)

7. Forgiveness – "If we confess our sins, He is faithful and just to forgive us our sins and cleanse us from all unrighteousness." 1 John 1:9 (MEV)

8. Reward – "May the Lord reward your deeds. May you have a full reward from the Lord, the God of Israel, under whose wings you have come to take refuge." Ruth 2:12 (MEV)

9. Punishment – "But he who does wrong will receive for the wrong which he has done, and there is no partiality." Colossians 3:25 (MEV)

The next revelation is the Spirits of God. Remember, God is three in one – God the Father, God the Son (Jesus) and God the Holy Spirit. Isaiah 11:1–2 speaks about the seven Spirits of God:

"And there shall come forth a shoot from the stump of Jesse, and a Branch shall grow out of his roots. The Spirit of the Lord shall rest upon him, the Spirit of wisdom and understanding, the Spirit of counsel and might, the Spirit of knowledge and of the fear of the Lord."

The Seven Spirits of God:

These are the spirits that not only identify who God is but are the spirits in which we should be transformed.

1. **Spirit of the Lord** – This is Jesus (Yahweh), the Name above all Names. He is God. He is the Son of God. He is Truth. He is without sin. He is the Lamb sacrificed for our sins. He is our Savior, our Healer, our Teacher, our Friend Who stands by

us and protects better than a brother, best friend, or lover. He is the Conqueror of eternal death. He is the Way to eternal life. He is our Peace, our Joy and our Hope. He is the Creator of life from the beginning of the world. He is a Miracle Maker. He is at the right hand of the Father. He is The Cornerstone – the first and most important stone placed for the foundation of God's kingdom. He is the First and the Last. He is ALL. This is the Spirit that indwells within us.

2. **Spirit of Wisdom** – God's wisdom is beyond our comprehension because he is all knowing. God knows the outcome of the decisions we make in our flesh (of our own accord). Not only does God know the immediate outcome, He knows the aftermath that will affect us and our family's future. God doesn't always reveal His reasoning behind the decisions He makes but we are to trust in Him and have faith that His decisions are what's best for us. This is why we should ask for Godly wisdom in regard to situations and decisions we need to make. God gives wisdom graciously to those who ask. Wisdom is the ability to make righteous decisions (decisions that align with God's will). Wisdom is pure, peaceable, gentle, open to reasoning, full of mercy and good fruits, impartial and sincere. (James 3:17)

3. **Spirit of Understanding** – God is the creator of all things. With that said, He not only understands how the world works, He understands you more than you understand yourself. God also has a greater understanding the evil Satan is capable of, creating wickedness in high places. God is the most intelligent Being in the universe! It would be unwise to NOT seek understanding from God. Godly understanding gives us discernment. It exposes evil. It gives us perspective. It helps us deal with difficult people and situations. It gives us confidence in Christ. It helps us to walk straight and not stumble. When we have Godly understanding, we are kinder, gentler, more peaceful and we have joy unspeakable. (Proverbs 3:13–24)

4. **Spirit of Counsel** – Unlike the counselors of this world, God is available 24/7, 365 days a year throughout the lifespan of a believer. God's counsel is truth and life. God is our advisor. He is our teacher. He guides us through difficult times because He is our coach and defender. God sees outside the circumstance and inside our inner being. There are many times throughout life in which sound advice is needed. There are also times in which situations are beyond mankind's comprehension.

You've heard people say, "I understand how you feel" or "I know what you mean" or "I get it." But they *don't get it.* Jesus told us it was better for Him to go because if he did not go away the Counselor would not come. Jesus was talking about the Holy Spirit; he is our Advisory, our Counselor.

When you don't have a resolution, when you don't know how to respond, when you are lost, when you are confused, when you don't understand, or when you feel alone and abandoned – PRAY and seek God's face.

Only God, the Holy Spirit, can convict someone of sin. Only God can bring someone to repentance. Only God can deliver a person from bondage. Only God can give a person peace in the midst of confusion. Only God can give joy to those infused with anger. Only God can replace hatred with love.

There are things beyond our capability. There is nothing too hard for God.

God calls those who are lost. God will give advice to those who hear. God will give direction to those who follow. God will deliver those who are sick of being stuck. God will give clarity to those who are confused. God's call is for all who are lost. God's will is dependent on our acceptance. (John 16:13–14)

5. **Spirit of Might** – God is mighty, but what does mighty actually mean? It means He has power, strength, victory, great achievements, political power, military force, power to liberate, splendor, valor, power of speech, strength in purpose and strength in affection.

Mankind cannot possess might without God; He is the one who strengthens us. When we look throughout the Bible, we can see amazing and mighty acts; yet not one was accomplished without the mighty power of God.

When Jesus was on earth, He accomplished many miraculous and mighty acts. Before Jesus left, He told us that WE will be able to do the things He did and even greater things, all in the Name of Jesus.

Yet we hang our heads in defeat when the enemy comes against us. We complain about impassable mountains. We become discouraged. We don't believe healing is for us.

When Jesus made the statement that we would do greater things (John 14:12– 14), He began by saying "truly, truly" (depending on the version you read, it could also say very truly or verily verily).

This means Jesus is serious, He is speaking truth, He has bolded and underlined His statement, He has placed millions of exclamation points behind His statement. It means BELIEVE ME WHEN I SAY!

God's Spirit of Might is available upon request, it is freely given to those who believe and to those who call on the Name of Jesus. Be a warrior for Christ! (Ephesians 6:10)

6. **Spirit of Knowledge** – God has the ability to know beyond human comprehension, He is all knowing; omniscient.

We've all had that friend or acquaintance who seems to have superhuman knowledge – in other words, they know everything. If you've had the pleasure of raising a teenage girl, then you know exactly what a 'know-it-all' really is.

Did you know there are several different types of knowledge?

a.   Preknowledge – this is the essence of reasoning power. It is knowing. Knowing is something not necessarily based on experience. For instance, if you looked out the window and saw the sun, you could deduce that it isn't raining outside.

b.   Post knowledge – this is gained knowledge; knowing something based on observation. If you looked outside the window and saw large low, dark clouds, you could safely say it will most likely rain nearby. This observation is based on gained knowledge.

c.   Explicit knowledge – this is head knowledge; knowledge that has been recorded and communicated through different means, such as a history book. Explicit knowledge is also knowledge that can easily be transmitted to other individuals by a mode of teaching.

d.   Tactic knowledge – this is aptitude knowledge; knowledge not only based on experience but a person's innate capability. God creates some people with unique capabilities. This type of knowledge is not easily communicated or transferred. It's only gained by blessing, constant exposure, and honed by teachings and relationships. For instance, a master musician cannot tell someone how to play an instrument, it requires teaching, studying, hours of practice, and a blessed aptitude.

e.   Propositional knowledge–this is declarative or descriptive knowledge. This is the knowledge of something, not the how-to. A good example would be memorizing the times table but not understanding the mechanics behind multiplication. Memorizing dates in history to establish a timeline is a good example of how to teach propositional knowledge when students have no concept of time or the context of dates in their geographical, cultural settings.

f.   Non-Propositional knowledge – this is procedural knowledge, the opposite of declarative knowledge. This is the act of understanding the mechanics behind something, the how-to. Instead of rote memorization, it's the knowledge of understanding and processing by faith, habit, or pattern based on experimental calculation of risk.

Using all types of knowledge for every situation and circumstance is beyond our ability, but not for God. Humans usually have a one-track mind; able to focus on two objectives at the same time at best.

God uses ALL aspects of knowledge for our good and for His glory. This is called revelation. God knows the reason. He knows the higher purpose. In providence, He observes and orchestrates all. He can create disaster, and He intervenes to redeem disasters and make them purposeful. He recorded and communicated His knowledge in the natural world in the history of nations and continents, and in scripture for revelation of Himself, His means, and His truth. God IS aptitude as He is love.

God can tell all about the mysteries of something hidden and He can divulge how-to.

Sometimes God will reveal things to us, but sometimes He won't. We should always pray and ask God to give us the knowledge we need. Regardless of whether He reveals what we need to know, we should lean on Him and trust His ways, His other servants, not our own understanding. (Proverbs 3:5–6)

7. **Spirit of the Fear of the Lord** – the ability to respect God's will and design. This is not an unholy fear; fear of rejection, fear of abandonment, fear of punishment, fear of death, fear of condemnation or fear of danger. There is no love in unholy fear and God IS love.

This is reverence for who God is, for what He is capable of, for what He has done and what He will do. This is the understanding that He is the Creator and King of the Universe. Angels sing, "Holy, Holy is the Lamb," without ceasing.

This is the absolute knowledge that He is eternal. This is thankfulness for His love, no matter what. This is awe of His mercy, grace and forgiveness – despite who we are. With this Holy Fear of the Lord we delight in obeying Him. We seek His face and His presence with anticipation. We are inspired by His beauty and His holiness. We pursue intimate instruction from Him. We are acceptant of His indwelling presence in our lives. We are pleased to walk beside Him and are excited to share Him with everyone. (Deuteronomy 10:12)

This is a lot to take in, but the revelation of who Jesus is in this passage is imperative to understanding the charge.

The seven stars are indicative of the control Jesus has with the angels. Jesus holds the destiny of the church in His hands. Regardless of a church's action, Jesus will be the final judge and jury.

COMMENDATION & CHARGE

"I know your works, that you have a name that you are alive, but you are dead." Rev. 3:1b NKJV

Jesus makes this short but sweet. He knows what the church has accomplished and even though it looks like they are flourishing, their spirit is dead. In essence, they are a pretend church. They go through the motions, keeping ceremonies and practices, yet they are not working in the Spirit of God.

Today's "church" is not complete.

World religions and even many churches don't work with all of God's tools in the fullness of the Lord, or in reverence of His authority and goodwill or providence.

Sometimes, a leader's lack of understanding will entice him or her to present to others the wrong conclusion or an ungodly option or position. Christians, there can be a lack of sacrifice, purification, and consecration in any human being.

Leadership requires meekness. Meekness is the sacred responsibility to walk with the Lord, to pray and listen, to wait for His counsel before spouting off what seems reasonable to human ears or denominational traditions.

Meekness is the ability to say, "I don't know, but let me ask the Lord," as Moses did when the five orphaned daughters of Zelophehad came to petition for their father's land in the face of a customary Jewish tradition to transition the responsibility and benefits of the land to the surviving male brother of the father. God gave Moses the wisdom to order the girls to inherit their father's land, but for the sake of tribal borders, in the event they chose to marry into another tribe, the land would not be assimilated by the other tribe. This decision was equitable for all.

Another clear example would be when forgiveness is given by the elders and their message is all about reward, yet they forget to speak of holy responsibility, eternal judgment, state or federal or church judgment, and natural consequences.

Unholy decisions and treatments of people's issues from those meant to watch over souls, do not come from the headwaters of God, or the spring of living water. They lack, simply, the power and authority of Jesus abilities when people defer to Him. Seek God's wisdom, understanding and knowledge whenever you don't know an answer. Relying on worldly counsel or identifying might in one's own strength can lead to wrong assumptions and delusionary habits that draw people down faulty roads, some roads which lead only to destruction.

What initially seems an inconsequential position can quickly turn into various forms of wickedness:

1. a calculated political maneuver that becomes more and more complex and spins out of control harming generations.

2. a decision to abandon a pregnant and unprotected girl, without the protection of God's people, can lead both she and her child to serious physical, psychological and spiritual risk.

3. a perversity of spiritual leadership creates a corrupt image of God in the pulpit.

It is interesting to see in the redemption of lives and restoration of parents to homes and workers to offices in the community, that the one thing God declines us to restore is the office of pastor to someone who has engaged in adultery. This is because the pastor stands in the position of a Shepherding God, a living motif of holiness and love, but when a pastor breaches that responsibility, the image of God is confused and perverted in many people's minds bring cringing dishonor to God and His covenant with believers. It makes mockery of Christians and their God. Since the despicable effect is broad, the discipline must also be broad and final. It is not that God removes the preaching gifts of the pastor, or other means of making a contribution to the community, earning a living, and finding redemption, but the office of shepherding others is not to be restored.

God restored David to kingship, but the epistles are clear when seeking a pastor, that the individual needs to be above reproach in the family, in the church, and even in the eyes of the community at large.

When there is no reverence for God, the local church operates like a carousel in the midst of a carnival going around and around instead of moving forward in God's authority imbued of truth and grace, prosperity and peace.

WARNING

"Remember therefore how you have received and heard; hold fast and repent. Therefore if you will not watch, I will come upon you as a thief, and you will not know what hour I will come upon you." Rev. 3:3 NKJV

There was a time in which the church heard and received the truth of the gospel. The church wholeheartedly repented and strived to be obedient to Christ. The church of Sardis asked for forgiveness and then walked away from the truth. Jesus is telling them to repent, return to true worship, to believe what His word says and live according to God's laws.

If they don't, they will not see the sign of the times. When the rapture comes, they will be asleep. They will be like the bridesmaids who didn't have enough oil in their lamps and missed the coming of the bridegroom.

They must incorporate the authority of the Lord along with God's wisdom, knowledge, understanding, counsel, might and reverence in order to stay awake.

ACTION NEEDED

"Be watchful and strengthen the things which remain, things that are ready to die, for I have not found your works perfect before God." Rev. 3:2 NKJV

Jesus is telling the church to WAKE UP! There are still aspects of their faith and ministry that are alive but they need to be serious.

The days of being a pew-warmer are over.

The days of checking the "I went to church" box are done with.

The days of listening and not practicing are ancient history.

The days of not studying God's Word have ended. The days of worshiping in the flesh and not in the spirit, have passed.

The days of not entering into intimate prayer with God, have concluded.

The days of not upholding true doctrine, are finished.

The days of not seeking a personal relationship with God, are gone.

It's DO or DIE.

ENCOURAGEMENT FOR THE OVERCOMER

"You have a few names even in Sardis who have not defiled their garments; and they shall walk with Me in white, for they are worthy. He who overcomes shall be clothed in white garments, and I will not blot his name out of the Book of Life; but I will confess his name before My Father and before His angels. He who has an ear, let him hear what the Spirit says to the churches." Rev. 3:4–6 NKJV

Not everyone in Sardis was pretending, there were a few who refused to be influenced by sin and had a genuine relationship with Christ. Jesus knows the names of those written in His book.

The Book of Life is a record of everyone who has been born once. The Lamb's Book of Life is a record of those who have been born twice, born from the womb then born again through the blood of Jesus Christ.

Jesus promises the ones who have not soiled their white garments (defiled their relationship with Christ by sinning and walking away) are worthy to be with Him and Jesus will acknowledge their salvation to the Father.

Don't you want your name to be presented to God? Imagine Jesus saying:

"Father, this is _____. I know him/her personally. He/She knows me as Savior, Counselor, and Friend. I died for his/her sins and he/she has accepted My payment to clean their slate of all legal and moral violation against You and Your holiness. In my own Name, Father-Judge, I present him/her to You, spotless and innocent."

Listen to the Lord for He has given you ears to hear. Remember His promises, repent for your sins and be righteous.

"For He made Him who knew no sin to be sin for us, that we might become the righteousness of God in Him." 2 Corinthians 5:21 NKJV

DAY ONE - PRAYER FOCUS

Repent for the times you didn't attune to the Spirit of the Lord– the divine nature and authority of Jesus Christ. Repent for the times you felt like Jesus wanted you to do something in His name and you questioned; for the times you did not operate in the authority He gave his believers; for not having faith in the Name above all Names.

Ask the Lord to excite your soul with the revelation of who Jesus is. Ask the Lord to help you have faith in knowing that Jesus has given you authority in His name to do the things He did and more. Ask Jesus to use you for His purpose and for the glory of God.

Scripture References:
James 4:17
Proverbs 16:20
Ephesians 1:17–23

DAY TWO - PRAYER FOCUS

Repent for the times you did not ask God for wisdom but operated on your own.

Ask the Lord to help you seek His wisdom above worldly wisdom. Ask the Lord to send helpers your way to confirm Godly wisdom. Ask the Lord to help you recognize the difference in between worldly wisdom and Godly wisdom (wisdom is pure, peaceable, gentle, open to reasoning, full of mercy and good fruits, impartial and sincere).

Scripture References:
James 3:17
Psalms 37:30
Ephesians 5:15–17

DAY THREE - PRAYER FOCUS

Repent for the times you did not reference God's word for understanding, for the times you may have walked in a path God had not ordained you to walk in because you failed to seek understanding. Repent for not having confidence in God.

Ask the Lord to help you seek His understanding more and more every day. Understanding God's design, purpose and will, helps you to recognize and resist evil; to walk and not stumble. Ask for an understanding that gives you a gentle spirit when dealing with difficult people or circumstances.

Scripture References:
Proverbs 2:2–5
2 Timothy 2:7
Jeremiah 33:3

DAY FOUR - PRAYER FOCUS

Repent for the times you did not call on the Lord for counsel. Repent for not hearing His advice, for not following His direction, for not allowing deliverance and not seeking understanding.

Ask the Lord to help you to seek His face and to understand that there are things beyond human capability. Ask the Lord to remind you that nothing is too big for Him.

Scripture References:
John 16:13–14
Psalms 16:7–8
Proverbs 8:14

DAY FIVE - PRAYER FOCUS

Repent for your unbelief in the mighty power of God. Repent for not moving forward when experiencing defeat in spiritual warfare, for complaining about impassable mountains or for becoming easily discouraged.

Ask the Lord to remind you daily that your strength is in Christ and that all things are possible in Him. Ask the Lord to show you His might through His word and the testimonies around you. Ask the Lord to help you become a mighty warrior.

Scripture References:
Ephesians 6:10
2 Samuel 22:33–37
Job 26:7–14

DAY SIX - PRAYER FOCUS

Repent for the times you acted like a 'know it all'. Repent for the times you became angry at God for not giving you revelation.

Ask the Lord to reveal reasons and observations that you cannot see. Ask the Lord to communicate His knowledge and to give you the aptitude to process the recorded word of the Lord. Ask the Lord to help you to not only know of something, but to be able to know how to. Ask the Lord to help you trust in Him always, even when He has not yet given you revelation.

Scripture References:
Proverbs 3:7
Proverbs 24:7
Ecclesiastes 7:12

DAY SEVEN - PRAYER FOCUS

Repent for the times you did not have full reverence for God. Repent for the times you thought of, or spoke about, the Lord as though he was just an acquaintance instead of the Holy God that He is.

Ask the Lord to help you respect His will and design. Thank the Lord for who He is, for what He is capable of, for what He has done and for what He will do. Thank the Lord and give Him praise for His mercy, grace and unwavering love. Take time to sing words of adoration "Holy, Holy is the Lamb of God".

Scripture References:
1 Chronicles 16:23–31
Jeremiah 20:13
Revelation 4:11

Chapter Seven

Faithful Followers

**'Only fear the Lord, and serve Him in truth
with all your heart; for consider what great things
He has done for you.'**
1 Samuel 12:24

Joseph was a beloved son. His father adored him.

His father clothed him in a colorful coat that made him stand out from the rest. God gave Joseph a designated purpose and the gift of prophetic dreams. The favor Joseph received from his father and the gift that God gave him, made others jealous and angry.

Those caught up in anger and jealousy rose up to kill Joseph, but God spared him because he had a purpose that even Joseph didn't understand. Joseph, the one who was loved and had favor, was sold into slavery. It didn't take long for Joseph to once again gain favor from his master, yet the enemy was determined to destroy Joseph.

Temptation flaunted itself in front of Joseph, but he was faithful to his master and ran from the temptation so he would remain innocent. His faithfulness should've been rewarded, but he was accused of a crime he did not commit and thrown into prison.

Joseph went from being loved to fearing murder, being betrayed, being sold into slavery, given favor, tempted by evil, wrongfully accused, then thrown away. It may seem like Joseph was cursed. But, God still had an door of opportunity awaiting him.

Instead of becoming angry and bitter, Joseph remained confident in the Lord. He was faithful, he stood firm on his beliefs, and he made the best out of every situation even in the most dire of circumstances. Joseph was given favor by God even within prison. God cared for him and Joseph became a prime example of Godly character, a foreshadow of Christ.

God cracked the door of opportunity and gave Joseph the gift of interpreting the dreams of his fellow prison mates. The only request Joseph made to the recipients of his gifts was to not forget him. When the cup bearer forgot, Joseph, still in prison, waited patiently, knowing that the Lord would soon come and release him.

God smiled upon Joseph's patience and faithfulness and gave Pharaoh a dream that no one could interpret. The cup bearer recalled his prison mate and told the Pharaoh. God's door of opportunity and purpose was wide open now. Joseph was called upon, cleaned up and presented to Pharaoh who told him of his terrible dream. Joseph did not deny God but gave God the glory of interpretation.

Pharaoh's eyes were opened to the wisdom God gave Joseph. Pharaoh acknowledged Joseph's God and gave Joseph a national position of authority above all in Egypt.

With Joseph's advice, the people were saved from a terrible famine. Pharaoh became abundantly prosperous during a time of depletion. Joseph's brothers bowed down to him and asked for forgiveness and then Joseph was reunited with his beloved father.

Because of Joseph's faith, obedience, patience, perseverance and wisdom, the Israelites were not only saved from extinction then, but continued to thrive beyond the Egyptians' ability to contain them.

The life of Joseph is a testament to what God expects from us. When we are faced with difficulties, when we are attacked by the enemy, when we are made out to be monsters, when life just doesn't seem fair – draw close to God.

Stand firm on His promises, walk in faith, do not deny the Lord your God, be determined to follow His laws, continue to work where God has placed you and be an example of Godly morals and character.

God will give you favor. He will never leave you. He will open doors of opportunity that will amaze even the unbelievers. Your Godly character will convict those who live in deception. And one day, God will make those who persecuted you stand and acknowledge that God is the one true God. They will bow down and exclaim that it was God who gave you favor because of His love for you. And you will be identified as God's own, the one who persevered and overcame. You will be gathered to a place that God has made for His faithful followers, the New Jerusalem, a place of security, peace and rest.

REVELATION OF JESUS

"And to the angel of the church in Philadelphia write, "These things says He who is holy, He who is true, He who has the key of David, He who opens and no one shuts and shuts and no one opens" Rev. 3:7 NKJV

Jesus is revealed as:

1. He Who is Holy

We know Jesus is holy, but what does that really mean? It means He is set apart (separated from sin, set above creation), He is sacred, and He is perfect. He is more than we can define.

2. He Who is true

Mankind sees truth as relative. It depends on the circumstance, the culture, the perspective, the outcome, or the views. It means nothing is ever true or false, good or bad, right or wrong – there is no absolute. There's no black and white; everything is blurred and confusing.

Mankind argues over truth. We argue about religion, politics, choices, history, education, and beliefs. Relativism is Satan's way of causing confusion and dissension.

Relativism is how he drives people away from God: if nothing is true or false, good or bad, right or wrong, then why should we obey, care, be concerned or believe in God? There is absolute truth, and His name is Jesus. Jesus is fixed, invariable and unaltered. He is the same yesterday, today and tomorrow. God's laws have not changed, God's purpose has not been altered, and God's plan is fixed.

Mankind accommodated sin to avoid Truth.

3. He Who Has the Key of David
Jesus, Who identifies Himself as "The One Who Holds the Key of David," has multiple meanings.

a. Fulfillment of the Davidic Covenant

The Davidic Covenant is an unconditional covenant that cannot be earned or removed based on man's works or obedience. To put it simply, it's a promise of an eternal seed (Jesus) that will come from the house of David. He will establish an eternal kingdom and He (Jesus) will govern from the eternal throne with authority forever.
2 Samuel 7:8–13 summarized states:

a. David was raised up from a shepherd to the ruler of Israel.

b. David is a victor over his enemies and his name is great.
c. God will establish a place for His people to dwell forever. They will move no more nor will they be afflicted by wickedness.
d. God will make the house of David great and a seed will be born from it.
e. God will establish a kingdom from the seed of David.
f. God will establish not only a kingdom, but a throne in which the seed will rule "from forever." This is a strange turn of phrase, but it wonderfully and mysteriously means the One Who is coming will be revealed to have existed from the beginning of time and will have been seated on His throne all along.

3   Absolute Authority

This next meaning ties into Jesus' proceeding comments about the opening and shutting.

Isaiah 22:20–23 speaks about stripping the treasurer and Shebna, the palace secretary, of their position and clothing Eliakim with a position of distinction. Eliakim will be well-liked and have a position of authority over the inhabitants of Jerusalem and the house of Judah. Eliakim would inherit the keys to the house of David — he would have ultimate authority.

When you look back on the scripture in Isaiah 22, you can see why authority was stripped from those in charge and given to someone with integrity and a zeal for God. Jerusalem was under siege, the rulers had fled, and the inhabitants were taken into captivity. Instead of turning to God during a time of unrest and turmoil, they partook of sinful activities — thinking they might as well indulge since they were going to die anyways.

4. He Who Opens the Door that No One Can Shut

An open door is an invitation and an opportunity. Jesus opened the door when He rose from the dead. It is meant for ALL to walk through and no one can shut it.

We may try to shut it, Satan may disguise it to look like it's shut, but Jesus says "come".

a. Jesus opens the door to faith.
b. Jesus opens the door to salvation.
c. Jesus opens the door to wisdom and understanding.
d. Jesus opens the door to ministry.
e. Jesus opens the door to righteousness.
f. Jesus opens the door to heaven.

That door will always be open. We can choose not to walk through it, but it can never be closed.

5. He Who Shuts and No One Opens

A closed door is a door we were not designed to go through, nor is it an opportunity for us to endeavor. God has given everyone a gift and a purpose to be used for His glory. Although the door is closed, it isn't locked. Sometimes we choose to walk through that closed door but our travel will not be blessed because God did not open the door for us.

COMMENDATION

"I know your works. See, I have set before you an open door, and no one can shut it; for you have a little strength, have kept My word, and have not denied My name." Rev. 3:8 NKJV

Again, Jesus talks about a door He has opened for the church and no one can shut it. The church of Philadelphia was a missionary church. They had little to work with, yet they continued with the mission God had given them.

The city of Philadelphia was noted as a city of many struggles. In 17 A.D., Philadelphia had a great earthquake that caused severe damage. But that wasn't all. The city endured daily tremors for many years. Structures collapsed and walls were severely cracked.

One part of the city would be damaged, then the next day another part would be damaged. People were afraid of the dangers within the city, so many lived outside of the city. The city couldn't prosper and was severely underdeveloped. The city also endured numerous Turkish invasions. Yes — they were small in stature, but mighty in faith.

Their perseverance and strong Christian beliefs eventually gained respect from the Turkish military.

Just like the church of Philadelphia, Christians endure many struggles. We are shaken by the social landscape. Sometimes those tremors are severe and other times they seem to be never-ending.

The media paints Christians as dangerous. Therefore, many avoid attending church or even question the existence of God. At times, Christians are under so much pressure they hide outside of their Christianity. They are afraid to rebuild what the enemy has torn down.

Although Christians have endured many attacks, we are to stay strong and never waiver from our beliefs and ministry. Keep true to God's word, never deny your faith in action or words and God will open doors that no man can explain or shut.

"Because you have kept My command to persevere, I also will keep you from the hour of trail which shall come upon the whole world, to test those who dwell on the earth." Rev. 3:10 NKJV

'Patience is a virtue' — we've all heard that saying and most likely, we've all quoted it. If we quote this saying incorrectly, we are in error. The truth is, 'Patience is a Christian virtue" that will be rewarded.

> Patience is endurance.
> Patience is determination.
> Patience is waiting.
> Patience is gentleness.
> Patience is love.
> Patience is faith.
> Patience is character.
> Patience is essential.

The church of Philadelphia suffered much, but they stayed patient in the Lord. They continued doing God's will while they bravely waited for Jesus' return. Because of their faithfulness, Jesus promised those who belonged to this church that they will not be part of the tribulation. They will not endure God's wrath.

Romans 1:18 tells us that God's wrath is for those who are ungodly, unrighteous and who suppress the truth (Jesus is truth).

Be like the church of Philadelphia. Stay true to God, be patient in the Lord, do not deny Jesus and walk in the ways of God so you will not see the tribulation.

THE CHARGE

Jesus did not charge the church of Philadelphia because they were the true church of Christ.

'There is therefore now no condemnation for those who are in Christ Jesus, who walk not according to the flesh, but according to the Spirit. For the law of the Spirit of life in Christ Jesus has set me free from the law of sin and death. ' Romans 8:1–2 MEV

The key here is 'those who do not walk in the flesh' and 'those that walk according to the spirit of Jesus Christ'. When there was no one left to condemn the adulterous woman, Jesus told her that He also did not condemn her, BUT he told her to go and sin no more. (John 8:11)

WARNING

"Indeed I will make those of the synagogue of Satan, who say they are Jews and are not, but lie - indeed I will make them come and worship before your feet, and to know that I have loved you." Rev. 3:9 NKJV

This warning is not to the church of truth but to those who defy the church of Christ. There are many churches that say they are Christians, but Jesus does not know them. They are liars, imposters and worshipers of Satan. There will come a time when those imposters will be repaid for their wicked deeds. They will bow down at the foot of the True Bride of Christ and acknowledge that Jesus is Lord.

These imposters are quick to hurl falsehoods towards Christians. It's become a sport for Satan to use the rebellious to deface Christians. He does this publicly so the whole world can see his ridicule of Christ. It's Satan's way to silence the True Bride of Christ, to make Christians suffer and to prevent the unsaved from ever knowing Christ as their Lord and Savior. Christians are taken to court, penalized for speaking about their faith, wrongfully accused when they stand against immorality, sentenced to death for believing in Christ and portrayed as haters.

Remember, Satan comes to steal, kill and destroy, (John 10:10). One glorious day, Christians will be exonerated for the whole world to see.

"Therefore God highly exalted Him and gave Him the name which is above every name, that at the name of Jesus

every knee should bow, of those in heaven and on earth and under the earth, and every tongue should confess that Jesus Christ is Lord, to the glory of God the Father." Philippians 2:9–11 MEV

ACTION NEEDED

"Behold, I am coming quickly! Hold fast what you have, that no one may take your crown." Rev. 3:11 NKJV

Jesus reminds us that His return will be as quick as the twinkling of an eye. A wink is approximately a half of a second long. A blink is 300 to 400 milliseconds, or about ¼ of a second long.

The twinkling of an eye refers to the reflected particle of light that we see in the eye. Since the speed of light is 186,000 miles per second, the twinkle of an eye is a billionth of a second — that's faster than processing a simple thought. There won't be time to ask for forgiveness, so the best course of action is stay ready at all times.

Hold on to the truth, don't walk away from the Lord's doctrine, keep doing God's work, evangelize, study and digest God's word, support God's mission and keep your transgressions short (ask for forgiveness immediately).

ENCOURAGEMENT FOR THE OVERCOMER

"He who overcomes, I will make him a pillar in the temple of My God, and he shall go out no more. I will write on him the name of My God and the name of the city of My God, the New Jerusalem, which comes down out of heaven from My God. And I will write on him My new name. He who has an ear, let him hear what the Spirit says to the churches." Rev. 3:12–13 NKJV

What a promise this is to the overcomer!

Pillar – the followers of Jesus will be made strong. They will be stable within God's house.

Go out no more – The church of Philadelphia understood this meaning all too well. Remember, they left the city because it was dangerous. Jesus is saying to his followers, no longer will there be danger for you; you will live in His security forever. You will no longer be subjected to wickedness and you will no longer hunger or cry. Death is wiped away and you will live in peace, love and joy all the days of your life.

Write the name – Jesus will write the Name of God (God's seal) that designates the follower as a child of God. The name of God's city (New Jerusalem) will be written on the follower to indicate them as a citizen of the re-created Jerusalem that comes from heaven down to earth after Satan is defeated. Jesus' new name will also be written on them as a witness that they have a personal relationship with the Lord.

Won't you have ears to hear this wonderful news?

"Then I saw 'a new heaven and a new earth.' For the first heaven and the first earth had passed away, and there was no more sea. I, John, saw the Holy City, the New Jerusalem, coming down out of heaven from God, prepared as a bride adorned for her husband. And I heard a loud voice from heaven, saying, 'Look! The tabernacle of God is with men, and He will dwell with them. They shall be His people, and God Himself will be with them and be their God. 'God shall wipe away all tears from their eyes. There shall be no more death.' Neither shall there be any more sorrow nor crying nor pain, for the former things have passed away.' He who was seated on the throne said, 'Look! I am making all things new.' Then He said to me, 'Write, for these words are faithful and true.'" Revelation 21:1–5 MEV

DAY ONE - PRAYER FOCUS

Repent for the times you didn't exhibit Godly character during times of trial. Repent for not making the best of a situation, no matter how bad it is.

Ask the Lord to help you to be like Joseph when trials come your way. Ask the Lord to help you to always look towards Him instead of looking at the circumstance. Ask the Lord to help you know that He is right there with you and even if you have to walk thru the fire, Jesus will hold your hand and give you a peace that passes all understanding.

Scripture References:
Philippians 4:8
Romans 5:3–5
2 Peter 1:5–7

DAY TWO - PRAYER FOCUS

Repent for the times you hid from your Christianity when those around you were either making fun of Christians or attacking them. Hiding from your Christianity could simply be not speaking up. Had Esther not spoken up and hid her Jewish roots, neither she, nor the Jewish race, would have survived.

Ask the Lord to give you a courageous spirit to righteously deal with friction and attacks from family, friends and social circles. Ask the Lord to use you as an example of what a Christian really is, so their perception is changed, and their hearts are open for salvation.

Scripture References:
Matthew 5:14–16
Esther 4:14
Romans 1:16–17

DAY THREE - PRAYER FOCUS

Repent for the times you either didn't notice the doors God opened, or you refused to walk through an open door. Repent for the times God called you to do a task, but you allowed fear and doubt to stop you.

Ask the Lord to give you more open door opportunities and the strength to walk through them. Ask for guidance and clarification on what He has called you to do. Ask the Lord for the confidence to do His will and to know that He equips those He has called.

Scripture References:
Ephesians 2:10
James 1:22
Ephesians 2:20–21

DAY FOUR - PRAYER FOCUS

Repent for the times you walked through a closed door, knowing it was not an opportunity God designed for you. Repent for following your flesh instead of seeking the will of God.

Ask the Lord to help you understand which doors are not meant for you — no matter how appealing or righteous they may seem. Ask the Lord to give you comfort and not confusion so that you can make Godly decisions based on His will and not your own.

Scripture References:
Proverbs 14:12
Proverbs 19:21
1 Corinthians 10:13

DAY FIVE - PRAYER FOCUS

Repent for the times you did not have patience, as God has designed patience.

Ask the Lord to help you endure and learn to wait on Him. Ask the Lord to help you desire to do God's will. Ask the Lord to help you walk in faith and to build Godly character while being patient. Let the Lord know how much you desire to see His coming, but you will enduringly wait in love, peace and gentleness for His return.

Scripture References:
James 5:7–8
Isaiah 40:31
Psalms 37:7–9

DAY SIX - PRAYER FOCUS

Repent for the times you felt hatred and anger towards those who oppose Christianity and attack Christians.

Ask the Lord to give you compassion for those people, instead of hatred. Ask the Lord to show you how He loves them and to know that God will defend Himself.

Scripture References:
Matthew 5:43–44
Romans 12:19–20
1 Peter 3:9

DAY SEVEN - PRAYER FOCUS

Repent for the times you did not pray for those who attack Christians or are deceived through false doctrines.

Ask the Lord to expose the lies of the enemy and to show you how you need to pray for those individuals.

Scripture References:
2 Corinthians 10:3–5
Colossians 3:13
Romans 12:21

Chapter Eight

Character of God

**"You are the salt of the earth.
But if the salt loses its saltiness,
how shall it be made salty?
It is from then on good for nothing but to be thrown out
and to be trampled underfoot by men."**
Matthew 5:13

Character is what a person is.

A person can have good character or bad character; either way, it reflects who they are as a person. Based on their character, you will know what they are about, what they believe and what they are capable of.

The character of a Christian should reflect the character of God in virtuous attitudes and actions. Christians strive to be:

1. Trustworthy
   a. Honesty with self and others
   b. Integrity throughout
   c. Reliability when times get tough
   d. Loyalty to God

2. Respectful
   a. Civil
   b. Courteous
   c. Forgiving
   d. Dignified

3. Responsible
   a. Accountable
   b. Pursue righteousness
   c. Exercise self-control

4. Caring
   a. Benevolent
   b. Charitable
   c. Sympathetic
   d. Loving
   e. Unselfish

5. Moral
   a. Good citizen
   b. Obedient
   c. Volunteer
   d. Committed

You will know who is safe to be around and who is dangerous, who you can trust and who to be cautious around.

Of course, every Christian is continually growing and maturing. We must also understand that all Christians are human and prone to sin – just like everyone else.

A true Christian recognizes their sinful nature – which is why they rely on, and devote themselves, to Christ. It's a lifelong process to adopt the character of God because we are not perfect as God is perfect.

A Christian's character can be injured by temptations and wrongdoing but thankfully the Lord's mercies are new every day.

REPUTATION IS WHAT OTHERS PERCEIVE ABOUT PEOPLE.

A Christian's reputation can be injured by slander, defamation, and malicious attacks. Satan will do all he can to ruin a Christian's reputation. He hones in on every temptation and wrongdoing and broadcasts it across society, usually blowing it way out of proportion.

Christians must understand that Satan possesses the opposite characteristics of God; therefore, he will be relentless, unforgiving, dishonest, disrespectful, callous, uncontrollable, hateful and immoral.

A Christian's reputation is under constant scrutiny, making it difficult to minister to the unsaved. The unsaved only need to hear one negative remark about a Christian or Christian group, to postulate a belief about all Christians.

Because of this, some Christians have become wishy-washy. It's hard to determine where they stand, what they are for and what they are against. They seem to be for everything and against nothing. They don't want to offend so they don't have an opinion. They welcome everything to avoid confrontation.

They are indifferent and have no character. At least with a true Christian, you know who they are as a person and what to expect from them. The same goes for a person against Christianity: you know who they are as a person and what to expect from them.

A wishy-washy person stands separated and in their own arena. What are they? Who are they? Are they safe or dangerous? Can you trust them, or should you be wary of them? What do they stand for? What do they believe?

They walk on the fence, unsure whether it's safe to walk on the green grass or be burned by the hot desert sand.

REVELATION OF JESUS

"To the angel of the church of the Laodiceans write: "The Amen, the Faithful and True Witness, the Beginning of the creation of God, says these things: Rev. 3:14 NKJV

For the final church, Jesus reveals Himself as an exclamation point. His existence is a loud sound of authority. His name invokes excitement and admiration. Every revelation of His name in this verse speaks of finality.

1. Jesus the Amen

There are many meanings and interpretations of the word "Amen" throughout the Bible. The most common use is after a prayer, meaning, 'So be it'.

Jesus used Amen frequently during His ministry on earth. Jesus' use of *Amen* spoke of authority and emphasized His deity. He has the authority to forgive sins, to judge and to perform miracles. *Amen* was used as a punctuation – meaning His words are truth, simply because He spoke them.

Other uses of *Amen* proclaim blessings or they mean to join in the praises of God (engage in worshipping God).

Although every one of these meanings describes the character of Jesus, the revelation of Jesus being The *Amen* means: Through Him the purposes of God are established. Jesus IS the fulfillment of the Law.

2. Jesus The Faithful

Jesus was faithful to do all God asked Him to do. He never sinned, although He was tempted. He is a perfect example of God's character. He loved everyone, yet never compromised the Law of God to please mankind.

Jesus The Faithful means He was steadfast and firm. He strictly observed God's Law. He was loyal and adhered to the facts, even when it wasn't the popular thing to do. Jesus will never change; His character will remain the same tomorrow as it was before the foundation of earth.

The greatest act of faithfulness was Jesus being tortured and brutally killed for the sake of those He loves (yes that means YOU) – despite knowing the pain and suffering He would endure.

Praise God!

Jesus was raised from the dead and accomplished all – it is finished!

3. Jesus The True Witness

Jesus is the witness that God is the great I AM. He, and He alone, is a witness to the fact that there never was, nor will there ever be, another 'god'. He is the savior; nothing else on this earth or above it can save you.

It is through the testimony of Jesus' life and resurrection that we are to know God is Who He says He is.

It has been declared and proclaimed that God was the beginning, and He is the end. No one can reverse what God has done and will do. He is our Creator and King. (Isaiah 43:9–13)

4. Jesus The Beginning of the Creation of God

Jesus was not created by God; we must make that clear. The definition of *beginning* means origin or source. (John 1:1–5) Jesus was there, Who always has been, and Who always will be. Jesus is God and He was there during creation – yet He still gives God the glory by identifying 'creation of God.'

If the Name above all Names, the King of Kings and Lord of Lords gives glory to God, shouldn't we?

COMMENDATION

- The loveless church of **Ephesus** was commended for their works, labor, patience, and the ability to not accommodate those who were evil. They were also commended for testing teachers and exposing those who taught lies.
- The persecuted church of **Smyrna** was commended for their works, even though they were in constant

tribulation. They lived in poverty and were constantly reviled by others.

- The compromising church of **Pergamum** was commended for their works even though they lived amongst evil people. They didn't deny Jesus or their faith, even when people were killed because of their beliefs.
- The corrupt church of **Thyatria** was commended for their works, love, service, faith and patience. They were also commended for moving forward with their ministry instead of becoming idle.
- The dead church of **Sardis** was not commended. They had a reputation of being alive, but they weren't. Jesus told them to repent because they were a pretend church; they were imposters.
- The faithful church of **Philadelphia** was commended for their works, even though they had little. They kept true to His word and never denied the name of Jesus.
- Then there is **Laodicea,** where there is neither a commendation nor an acknowledgement of any reputation.
  - o Laodicea was a commercial and industrial city that manufactured many well sought-after goods. A strange thing, they were known for their lukewarm water. Their hot water was piped in from somewhere south of the city, but by the time it reached Laodicea, it was no longer hot. They were also the home to a school of medicine in which physicians created ointments by mixing foreign compounds in hopes of curing collective diseases.
  - o Even with these characteristics, there was nothing about Laodicea that stood out; they were mediocre citizens living a ho-hum lifestyle. The city had a mixture of numerous nationalities and religious beliefs.

- Laodicea's citizens were tolerant of everything and anything. There were no struggles, contentions, picket lines or riots amongst the people. They were well-ordered and energetic about commercialism, but the people were cold-natured and misdirected in their understanding of their liberty.
- They lacked self-sacrifice and enthusiasm for Christ.

Jesus had nothing good to say about Laodicea. He insults them by calling them poor, blind, and naked, exactly the opposite of their branding. You would think that would scare them into at least searching for enthusiasm, but it was like water on a duck's back to them. Lukewarm water, that is. Jesus had nothing good to say about Laodicea. He insults them by calling them poor, blind, and naked, exactly the opposite of their branding. You would think that would scare them into at least searching for enthusiasm, but it was like water on a duck's back to them. Lukewarm water, that is.

THE CHARGE

"I know your works, that you are neither cold nor hot. I could wish you were cold or hot. So then, because you are lukewarm, and neither cold nor hot, I will vomit you out of My mouth.' Rev 3:15–16 NKJV

Have you ever met someone with no desire, passion or interest? We're not talking about depression. This is much worse than depression.

These people just go through the daily motions. They don't move forward, they don't even move backwards; they stand still, unchanged. They wake up, get dressed, go to work (if they even work), come home, eat dinner then go to bed – only to repeat the same actions the next day.

'What's the point?' is their motto. That's not only what they feel, it becomes who they are. They are hopeless, apathetic, indifferent and unconcerned. They neither have a like nor a dislike.

Ask an apathetic person what they like to do and they won't have an answer. It isn't because they're lazy, they honestly don't know what they like.

Ask an apathetic person what they like most about themselves or dislike about themselves, and they won't be able to answer you. They are emotionless; they are neither dead nor alive. They are lukewarm.

Sounds like a terrible state of being, doesn't it? So was the lukewarm church of Laodicea.

COLD CHURCH!

A cold church is void of true spirituality. They arrive and go through the motions. Their services are monotone, their music is lifeless, and they don't encourage people to have a personal relationship with Christ.

There's no spiritual growth, no outreach ministry, no dedication and no congregational involvement. An individual's attendance is sporadic; they come when they feel like it and their absence goes unnoticed.

They accept worldly practices, not setting themselves apart as Christ requires. A cold church may have a large congregation because there's no conviction. It's Sunday social hour and nothing more. The good news is, a cold church can experience revival and be reborn.

HOT CHURCH!

A hot church is passionate and on fire for God. They are eager to go whenever the church doors are open. Their services are full of life, worship is powerful, and the congregation strongly desires a close relationship with Christ.

Their growth may not be in numbers, but in souls and spirituality. They support numerous missions and look for ways to reach out into the community. The congregation is dedicated to Christ and they love to fellowship with each other.

When someone misses a service, everyone notices. They are convicted to continue walking in God's will and to follow God's commandments. Their passion and excitement can minister to even the coldest of hearts.

LUKEWARM CHURCH!

A lukewarm church is indifferent to spirituality and accepts what is unacceptable to God. They state with their mouth that they are Christians, but they are imposters.

Just like the cold church, they arrive and go through the motions. But their services and worship may be governed by a strict schedule. The congregation looks forward to the events after church more than going to church itself.

They walk the walk and talk the talk but once they leave the church, their lifestyle reflects something completely different. They are hypocritical, self-sufficient, and wealthy.

Not only is the majority of the congregation on the fence about Christianity, they are also overly liberal and allow people to become leaders whose lifestyles reflect rebellion towards God. They don't feel the need to have a personal relationship with Christ; going to church is all that's required of them.

They have no appetite for growth, either individually or as a whole. They are prone to adopt numerous doctrines or create ones of their own. They're not sure if the Bible is completely true; therefore, following the commandments is more of a suggestion than a requirement. They live like everyone else in the world and are indifferent to Christian morals; what's good for the goose is good for the gander. They glorify themselves instead of glorifying God. They are complacent and perfectly comfortable being who they are. Jesus says He will vomit the lukewarm church out of His mouth – which doesn't paint a pretty picture. What can Jesus do with an apathetic church? If they were cold, He could convict hearts to excite them into revival. If they were hot, He would give them more passion and desire.

But an indifferent and apathetic church?

WARNING

'Because you say, 'I am rich, have become wealthy, and have need of nothing' — and do not know that you are wretched, miserable, poor, blind, and naked — I counsel you to buy from Me gold refined in the fire, that you may be rich; and white garments, that you may be clothed, that the shame of your nakedness may not be revealed; and anoint your eyes with eye salve, that you may see. '
Revelation 3:17–18 NKJV

Jesus never asked a church to become rich and acquire as much as they can in order to be acceptable. Jesus, the King of Kings and Son of God, came as a servant. He was born in a stable, not a palace.

This church, like many churches today, felt they needed nothing else because they were rich. When they looked in the mirror the reflection, they saw was fortunate, satisfied, rich, understanding and robed in righteousness. But they were looking into the mirror of deception.

Jesus says, 'look into the mirror of truth, and you will see yourself as wretched, miserable, poor, blind and naked'.

Their so-called riches (gold) were unpurified and dirty, just as their lives were unrighteous and unacceptable to God.

God says to purchase His gold; gold that has been refined by the fire, pure gold.

This is not a special currency God wants to give the church; it's the most precious and purest gift God has ever given – His son Jesus Christ.

Through this purchase, one will receive salvation. And with salvation they will be given a white robe to signify their purity. This robe will cover their transgressions. Once robed with righteousness, the Holy Spirit can open their eyes to the truth and the truth will set them free.

ACTION NEEDED

"As many as I love, I rebuke and chasten. Therefore, be zealous and repent. Behold, I stand at the door and knock. If anyone hears My voice and opens the door, I will come into him and dine with him, and he with Me." Revelation 3:19–20 NKJV

An unloving parent allows their children to do whatever they want, whenever they want. A loving parent has no problem telling their child "*NO*" to teach them a lesson, or to help them learn the difference between right and wrong, or keep them safe from danger. When the child grows up, he or she will know to stay away from danger, and wise decisions will be within reach.

Just like a parent, God's love does not come without discipline when we disobey. Godly discipline brings us to repentance and teaches us the difference between right and wrong. The concept is for us to learn through this process and to keep us from continually sinning.

God knows we aren't perfect, and He knows we will sin, but He doesn't want us to have a 'what's the point' attitude. God asks us to have a desire and passion for Him. When we long to please God, we are diligent to repent.

Regardless of what we choose to do, Jesus is there knocking on the door. He isn't demanding us to come to Him, nor is He begging and pleading. Jesus is already there – knocking. It's up to us to open the door and invite Him into our heart.

Imagine a family eating at the dinner table. What do you see? They're sharing food, talking about their day, encouraging one another, solving problems, laughing and having a great time of fellowship and bonding. Jesus' dining with us and us dining with Him, is the same thing.

At Jesus' dining table the word of God is shared, and we are fed. We talk about our day and Jesus gives us encouragement. Jesus helps us with our problems. There are times when we laugh together and just have a great time of fellowship. We draw closer and form a long-lasting relationship.

ENCOURAGEMENT FOR THE OVERCOMER

'To him who overcomes I will grant to sit with Me on My throne, as I also overcame and sat down with My Father on His throne. "He who has an ear, let him hear what the Spirit says to the churches.' Revelation 3:21–22 NKJV

Jesus is the overcomer; He has conquered death and the grave. He currently sits on the throne at the right hand of the Father. Jesus was placed in a position of prestige. Jesus wants us to accept Him, love Him and be obedient to Him. When we do this, we are also overcomers and Jesus will give us a place of prestige in Heaven. We will reign with Him.

"For whoever is born of God overcomes the world, and the victory that overcomes the world is our faith." 1 John 5:4 MEV

DAY ONE - PRAYER FOCUS

Repent for being idle.

Ask the Lord to give you strength to continue doing the work He has assigned you to do. Ask for revelation so you know what God has asked you to do.

All Christians are asked to work for the Lord, and all have been given a purpose and assignment. Ask the Lord to help you move one foot in front of the other so you can continue the race.

Scripture References:
Proverbs 19:15
1 Timothy 5:13
Galatians 6:9

DAY TWO – PRAYER FOCUS

Repent for thinking the knowledge you have is sufficient. Repent for not continuing to learn more about God.

Ask the Lord to help you continue to grow. Ask the Lord to give you a stronger desire to know more and increase your understanding of Him.

Scripture References:
2 Peter 3:18
Proverbs 1:5
Jeremiah 9:23–24

DAY THREE - PRAYER FOCUS

Repent for not seeking the Lord because you feel you are spiritually satisfied.

Ask the Lord to have His spirit become more alive within you. Ask the Lord for more passion towards Him so it never ceases but increases.

Scripture References:
Matthew 5:6
Isaiah 26:9
Psalms 63:1

DAY FOUR - PRAYER FOCUS

Repent for feeling fortunate and abundant. This could be materialistic, spiritual, wisdom, triumph over trials or your Christianity in general.

Ask the Lord to take away the mirror of deception and replace it with the mirror of light and truth. Ask for humility. Be reminded that the Lord gives, and the Lord takes away. You don't count your worth based upon a) what you have acquired or b) your trials in life.

Scripture References:
Isaiah 47:10
Galatians 6:3–5
1 Peter 5:6

DAY FIVE - PRAYER FOCUS

Repent for having a 'what's the point' attitude.

Ask the Lord to help you see purpose and to know there is a reason for the season. Ask the Lord to change your attitude; let it always point to the hope and salvation in Christ and not on what we feel we cannot do, or what will not happen.

Scripture References:
Romans 8:18–19
2 Corinthians 4:8–10
Romans 8:37–39

DAY SIX - PRAYER FOCUS

Repent for having no passion or appetite for growth.

Ask the Lord to show you the areas in which you can grow. Ask for growth in your personality, ministry, relationships with others, relationship with Christ, talents, tasks and evangelism.

Scripture References:
Psalms 84:1–2
Galatians 4:18
1 Corinthians 14:12

DAY SEVEN - PRAYER FOCUS

Repent for not dining with the Lord.

Ask the Lord to help you make time to dine with Him. Let the Lord know how much you desire to bond with Him, to laugh with Him, to have a conversation with Him about your day. Let Him know you long for his encouragement and companionship.

Scripture References:
Psalms 23:5–6
Luke 14:15
Songs 2:4

CONCLUSION

The letters to the seven churches are not just for the past; they are for the present and the future. Backsliding, persecution, compromise, adultery, pretending, and apathy are alive and well in the church today. This means individuals and the church as a whole. The charges and warnings are a serious matter, and we must be intentional, obedient, and vigilant.

This is not a one-and-done study. Come back and review so you will continue to labor for God. Be patient. Increase your discernment by staying in His word. Test teachings and doctrines against God's word and reject those that are false. When you have little or are persecuted, stand firm, and don't deny Jesus Christ. Work in love and walk in faith. Don't become idle. Continue to move forward so you are doing greater things than before. Never stop drawing closer to God and you will be an overcomer.

"I press toward the goal for the prize of the upward call of God in Christ Jesus." Philippians 3:14 NKJV

About the Author

Sheri Caruso is a Woman's Ministry leader, Author and Speaker.

She lives in Colorado with a loving husband, 4 children, 3 stepchildren, 8 grandchildren, 3 horses, 20+ chickens (include one attack rooster), 2 goats and 3 dogs – Sheri is certain one of the dogs is a spawn of gremlin.

Sheri is the daughter of pastor and missionary, Rev. Joseph & Jennifer Comer Sr. Her late father was one of the pastors to plant churches in Korea. He taught himself how to read, write and speak Korean so he could effectively preach the word of God. Sheri actively serves in her home church and where called to speak.

Sheri's husband is Joe Caruso (adding a third Joe to the family due to both her father and brother's names being Joe). He is the Vice-President of a home design company. He is also actively serving in their home church as a Sunday school teacher and board member. Joe may not be famous, but he is famously the apple of Sheri's eye.

Though Sheri was nurtured in church, she experienced such personal troubles that her heart for the brokenhearted was formed. Her passion is to help those who feel hopeless and lost experience God's grace and mercy. It's available to all, despite what has transpired in the past. Sheri's testimony is a remarkable example of how God can redeem and restore the lowliest individual.

You can find Sheri here to read devotional blogs, hear about new book releases, projects and speaking engagements.
Shericaruso_author@yahoo.com
Facebook: www.facebook.com/shericarusoauthor
Website: https://shericaruso.com

About Sackcloth and Ashes of the Heart

Is it time? Are we there yet? How much longer?

With the rapid decay of society's morals and ethics, these questions resonate throughout the church body. Lord? Is it time for your return? Lord? Are these really the end times? Lord? How much longer? Lord…come…even now!

Although our bags are packed as we anxiously await Jesus' return, we must honestly ask ourselves, "Am I truly ready? Am I prepared to see Jesus, face to face? Will I be counted approved for His return?" Our first instinct is to say "Yes! Yes, I am ready!" But are you?

Sackcloth and Ashes of the Heart's purpose is to restore the true church of Jesus Christ by:

- Reviving our hearts with a supernatural love,
- Giving us strength in a world full of evil,
- Realigning our doctrine back to truth,
- Exposing evil within our congregations,
- Keeping us connected to God's headship,
- Being teachable as faithful followers – regardless of our situation,
- And instilling God's character in every aspect of our lives.

This 8–week study takes you through a comparative journey of today's church and the seven churches in Revelation. We will reveal who Jesus is, explore His commendations, relate the charges Jesus had against the church to the churches of today, heed His warnings, and be intentional to strategize for the actions we must take so we can stay intentional and faithful in the course our race and receive the rewards Jesus has for all those who overcome.

There are daily prayers of repentance throughout this study – after all, that is the focus of this study: to reveal, repent and restore.

The hour of Jesus' return is drawing near and its time we become distraught over the condition of our society and the church. It's time we become uncomfortable sitting in our padded pews and prostrate ourselves before the Lord.

Are you ready? Are you truly ready for Jesus' return? Instead of wondering, take this journey of repentance and be restored!

"Restore us again, O God, and cause Your face to shine, and we shall be delivered."
Psalms 80:3 MEV

CPSIA information can be obtained
at www.ICGtesting.com
Printed in the USA
LVHW111932120521
687238LV00005B/274

9 781951 084424